Circular Walks Around
MIDHURST

MICHELE FACER

FINDING
FOOTPATHS

All walks have been carefully checked prior to inclusion in this book. The author can accept no responsibility for harm encountered as a result of following the walking routes. Walkers are responsible for their own safety, and are encouraged to familiarise themselves with the guidance given in The Countryside Code.

First edition MARCH 2022

Cover design by CLAIRE SMITH
Proof reading by MADDY GLENN
Design and layout by JULIA HUGHES
Printed by TJ Books, Padstow

ISBN 978-1-5272-9395-3

findingfootpaths.com

CONTENTS

FOR MUM

FOREWORD

In Old English, the word 'Midhurst' means place among the wooded hills. It is a fitting name for a town that is so neatly nestled in some of the most beautiful countryside that Southern England has to offer.

Many centuries after it was first named, the hills are still wooded, still gently wrapping themselves around the town, as if to protect it. On lower slopes and in river valleys, the patchwork patterns of farmland are reminders of a medieval past. Wildlife thrives, nurtured by habitats that have many more miles of hedgerows and quiet footpaths than roads.

This is a soft and tranquil landscape, deep in the heart of the South Downs National Park, which has long since been recognised for its natural beauty. Its inclusion in the National Park gives much needed protection, for there are rare species, ancient grasslands, and internationally acclaimed dark skies to be found here. Visitors are drawn to the wide-open spaces that feel deliciously distant but, in reality, aren't that far from the large towns and cities of South-East England.

DISCOVER A WORLD BEYOND THE DOWNS

The South Downs Way passes close by as it follows its chalk ridge from Winchester to Eastbourne. Along its entire length, there are stunning views, and the area around Midhurst is no exception. From this popular trail you can see beyond the town to the Western Weald, a large expanse of woodland and heath that, in turn, provides exceptional views back towards the Downs. This weald is also part of the National Park. With footpaths that are quiet and sheltered, it makes a pleasing contrast to the busier and more exposed terrain of the Downs.

With the Weald to the north, Downs to the south, and farmland to the east and west, Midhurst is quite literally surrounded by countryside. In every direction there are endless, well-maintained footpaths. You can walk for 10 or even 20 km before encountering another town.

There are villages and country lanes to discover but few major roads to interrupt your rambles. It is a landscape that cries out to be explored on foot, and that is the point of this book. Using Midhurst as a base, and the book as a guide, you can walk the woods and hills that gave the town its enduringly appropriate name.

INTRODUCTION

There are eight walks in this guide. All are circular, starting and ending at Market Square in Midhurst.

The routes are designed in a way that enables them to be adapted. You can follow them as written or make them longer or shorter to suit your needs. The aim is to encourage 'on foot' exploration. If you live in Midhurst, leave your car at home. If you live further afield, leave your car in one of the large car parks. This is far easier than relying on smaller rural parking areas, laybys, or verges. Better still, leave the car at home and travel by bus. There are regular services from Chichester, Petersfield, Haslemere, and Bognor Regis.

In between the walk descriptions, there are features on local businesses that you might find interesting and useful. These are not the usual 'where to stay' or 'where to eat' recommendations, nor are they paid-for advertisements. They are an invitation to hear the stories behind the independent businesses that help give Midhurst its character. Expect to learn a little about the town through the eyes of the people who have carved out a living here. Some have been here all their lives, some are new arrivals, but all have a story to tell.

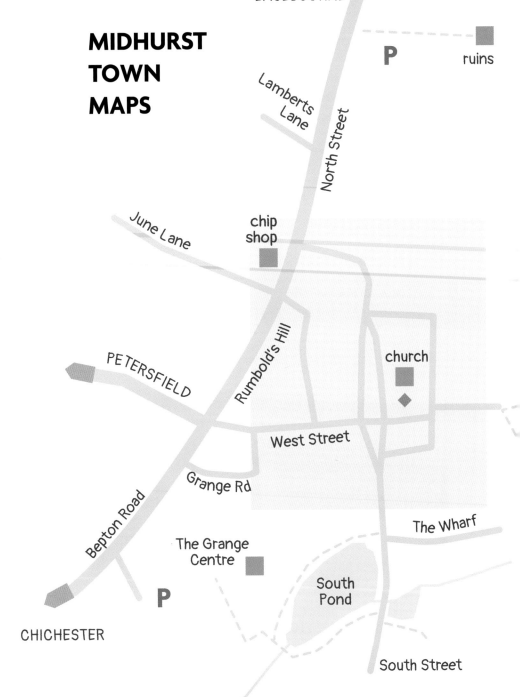

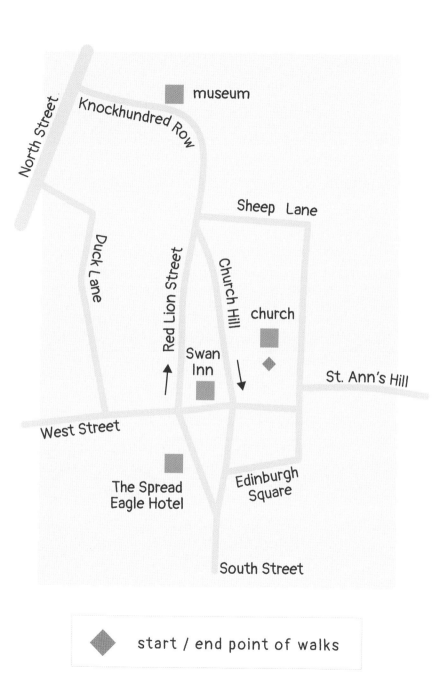

museum

North Street

Knockhundred Row

Sheep Lane

Duck Lane

Red Lion Street

Church Hill

church

Swan Inn

St. Ann's Hill

West Street

The Spread Eagle Hotel

Edinburgh Square

South Street

◆ start / end point of walks

WHO IS THIS GUIDE FOR?

Anyone looking to get outdoors and explore, to be surrounded by beautiful scenery or an abundance of wildlife will be able to make good use of this book. Its purpose is to inspire, to guide, and to stimulate your appetite for walking via the descriptions and imagery it presents.

It is for those who enjoy having options and the ability to return to much-loved walks. Varying the route to suit mood or weather. Visiting often, but always seeing something different, as the ever-changing seasons make their impact on the land. Midhurst is an excellent place to find such options. Its network of footpaths offers endless walking possibilities that will keep you coming back for more, time and again.

KEEP IT SHORT AND SWEET

Those new to walking can rely on the detailed route guides to support them. There is no need to worry about map reading or navigation. Every walk has at least one short option that will cater for the lightest of walking appetites. Follow the walks in sequence to build your experience and stamina. Repeat them as often as you can to feel confident in different weather conditions and seasons. Above all, enjoy them as you cultivate your taste for the outdoors.

TAKE YOUR TIME, STAY OUT ALL DAY

Experienced walkers will enjoy the longer routes, and extensions. This guide is an invitation to walk at length. You are encouraged to adapt the routes and create new variations that you can call your own. There are numerous places and trails to explore within a 15–20 km radius of Midhurst, and not every walk has to be circular.

There are good local bus services, which give plenty of scope to do without your car. Use this guide to inspire you to seek out new ways of getting from place to place on foot, linking footpaths together in creative ways to visit every corner of this beautiful place.

Finally, there are those who prefer to walk vicariously. If this is you, feel free to simply enjoy the photography and prose. Give yourself the illusion of an outdoor experience without having to leave the comfort of your sofa. Maybe consider trying a short walk or two. You might be surprised by how much there is to be gained from being outdoors, surrounded by nature and away from all the usual demands on your time.

WHAT DO I NEED?

There is not much by way of specialist equipment needed to walk the footpaths around Midhurst. Elevations are not high enough to hijack your walk with unforeseen bad weather. Even the steepest slopes can be safely navigated all year round.

Although you can find solitude, you'll never be too far from someone who can help you. Network coverage is good on almost every part of each route. However, an additional battery pack is a wise investment if you have any concerns about your phone holding its charge, especially on a longer walk.

Your biggest enemy will be mud. Sussex is known for it. Even on the driest of summer days, you can still come across it, and walking with wet feet is not fun. A good pair of comfortable shoes or boots will serve you well, especially if they are waterproof. In winter, wet footpaths become slippery, so a stick or walking poles can be helpful, particularly if you have any concerns about your knees or back.

A waterproof jacket is always going to be useful if the weather is unsettled. Even if rain is not forecast, you will find it a great defence against wind. Unlike some of the more remote and unpredictable landscapes in the UK, you can generally leave waterproofs behind when the forecast is good.

Whilst there are some excellent pubs and cafés in Midhurst, there are few amenities along the routes, so you do need to be prepared to take food and drink with you. A rucksack is by far the best way to carry this when you're walking.

LET'S TALK ABOUT MAPS....

You might enjoy following the walks on a commercially produced map. You will almost certainly need one if you are planning to follow the suggested variations or make your own adaptations. You can access digital maps on the move using applications like Outdooractive or OS Maps. If you prefer a physical copy, you would do well with one that is a 1:25 000 scale.

Ordnance Survey produce a range known as the 'Explorer Maps', which provide an ideal level of detail for walkers. OL33 covers about half the walks in this book, with OL8 and OL10 covering the rest.

A really useful alternative is a custom-made Explorer Map that is centred on Midhurst. This will cover all the walks in this book, and is much easier to use than navigating across multiple maps. You can order a custom map from the Ordnance Survey website.

FOREST OPERATIONS

Be aware that much of the woodland around Midhurst is actively managed. This means that trees are cut down on a regular basis. It is a necessary activity that maintains the overall health of the woods. When walking, you need to pay attention to warnings of 'Forest Operations'. Be ready to adapt your route if needed. Recently felled areas are going to look a bit different from the descriptions in this guide. You may also find that footpaths have been buried under debris or vehicle tracks. If this happens, it is useful to have access to paper or digital maps so that you can navigate around these areas.

The one thing you really do need is a willingness to believe in the positive power of walking. To walk is to give yourself an opportunity to free your mind and soothe your soul. You may be alone or with others. You might go for miles or just a short stroll. Whatever you choose to do, you will find yourself making a connection with nature that is guaranteed to boost your energy levels and lift your spirits.

The more you get outdoors and explore, the greater the benefits will be to your health, wellbeing, and confidence. This is the power of walking. We don't need research to confirm it. Instinctively, we know it to be true. Many people tap into this power on a daily basis, and if you're not yet one of them, use this book to help you get started. All you have to do is open your mind, open your door, and step outside.

1

PART ONE

GETTING STARTED

Not much of a walker? Worried about getting lost? Convinced you'll end up with blisters? Fear not! The walks in the first part of this book are straightforward and enjoyable.

They take advantage of the fact that Midhurst is a compact town surrounded by beautiful countryside. Each route has at least one option that will take less than 2 hours to complete. If you want to be out for longer and explore further, just follow the route as written and consider including one or more of the suggested extensions.

YOU CAN DO THIS....

If you are feeling doubtful about your ability to get outdoors and walk, take a look at the image opposite. It shows an Edwardian family in 'The Severals', which is a pine forest you can explore in Walk Three. Reflect for a moment what it might have been like to go walking back then.

Today, we have access to clothes that are designed to support active lives, comfortable shoes, and mobile phones for emergencies. Our Edwardian predecessors managed to walk for pleasure in this place with none of these items. If they did it, you can definitely do it too.

THE ONE WITH THE RIVER

This walk follows a well-signposted route called the 'Rother Walk', which was created jointly by the National Trust and the South Downs National Park. At the edge of town, where Midhurst meets Easebourne, pick up this footpath and follow it through woodland and farmland, tracking the river's course out towards Woolbeding.

Almost as soon as you set foot on this path, it is as if you have closed a door on the world. The woodland envelopes you, swapping traffic noise for birdsong. You will wonder how it can be true that a thriving town lies so close, just beyond the trees. Despite its proximity to Midhurst, you are in an un-tamed landscape. There is no charming promenade alongside this river. Nature is in charge, and wildlife flourishes as a result.

You will loosely follow the course of the river for about 1.5 km before reaching Woolbeding Parkland. As you emerge from a small wood at the top of the hill in the middle of the park, you are treated to some expansive views that reach all the way to Beacon Hill on the South Downs. Behind you, Woolbeding House and All Hallows Church nestle into the landscape just the other side of the river.

After exiting the parkland, there is a short stroll along a minor road before you can join another footpath to take you across the gently sloping fields to the rear of Midhurst Rother College and back to North Street, where you can grab an ice cream or a coffee before heading back to the starting point.

WALK ONE
➡ 5 km / ⧖ 1½ hours

THE ONE WITH THE RIVER

Woolbeding House and Gardens

Half Moon pub

A272

PETERSFIELD

Midhurst Common

	route guide		walk route
	woods		alternative route
	site of interest		footpath/track
P	parking		road

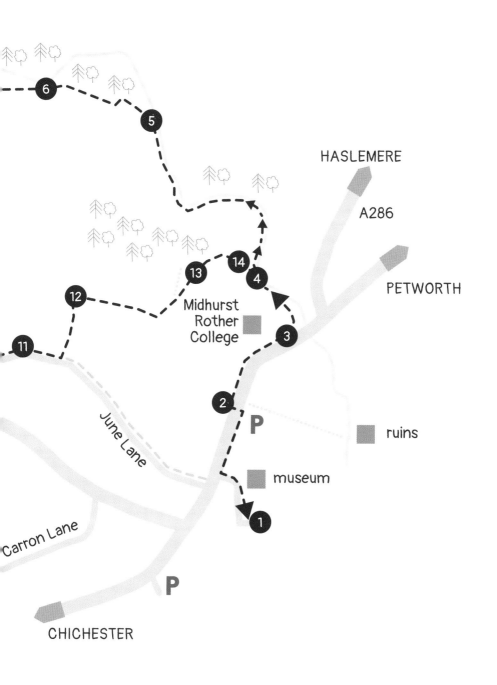

⮑ VARIATIONS

At just under 5 km, this is a fairly short route. However, as you near the end of it, you could remain on the road rather than taking the footpath across the fields (Point **11.**). This is a helpful variation if the weather has been wet, as this footpath can sometimes be quite muddy. By continuing down June Lane, you'll arrive in town close to the Ocean Blue Fish & Chip shop, making the route easier and shorter. Another option is to walk as far as the boardwalk (Point **5.**) and then back to town again. This is a pleasant stroll that can be completed in less than 1 hour.

If you are looking for ways to make the walk longer, a good option is to cross the A272 as you emerge from Woolbeding Parkland (Point **9.**) to make your way onto Midhurst Common. This area is full of footpaths, and to help you navigate them, an additional sketch map is provided. Exploring this area, you will find lakes formed from old clay pits, white sandy beaches, and lots of clues to the railway lines that used to be a feature of this landscape.

When you are done exploring, you can exit the common at various points on Carron Lane for a short walk on residential streets back to town, or you can trek a bit further across the common to emerge on Bepton Road, turning left to head back to town. If you are going to explore, it's worth using a digital map to track your location. It is surprisingly easy to lose your way on woodland trails.

MORE RIVER PLEASE

If you are keen to get closer to the river, there is an option to remain on the lower ground as you enter Woolbeding Parkland. There is a faint, unmarked path that leads around the bottom of the hill, and beside a small lake before re-joining the main route (Point **8.**). This variation is described below and is also shown on the route map. Note that it can be extremely boggy. Ensure you have suitable footwear or wait until there has been a period of dry weather before attempting this variation.

⮂ AMENITIES

There are plenty of shops, pubs and cafés in Midhurst but only one pub along the route. Plan carefully, particularly if you are walking with children. Take plenty of water with you. Even though this route is short, on hot days it can be a real sun trap.

⮂ ROUTE GUIDE

1. Facing the Swan Inn with the church to your right, make your way from Market Square to North Street by turning right onto Church Hill to walk past the church, several houses, and the Midhurst Museum. When you reach the junction with North Street, turn right and make your way past the shops to the second of two pedestrian crossings.

2. Cross over the road and continue to head away from town, passing the South Downs Centre, Methodist church, and the main entrance to Midhurst Rother College on your left. Just after the crossing, note the blue plaque on the wall of what was Midhurst Grammar School. It marks the fact that H.G. Wells was both a pupil and a teacher here. On the opposite side of the road are the ruins of Cowdray House, which features in Walk Two.

3. Ahead, there is a bridge over the river and a sign for Easebourne. Before you get to this, turn left to follow a footpath between the trees and towards the weir. With the weir ahead of you, the footpath turns sharply to the left to follow a small water-filled channel parallel to the river. With this channel on your right, follow the path, ducking slightly to pass under a pipe that crosses at head-height in front of you.

4. After 100 m, the path forks. Bear right to come to the edge of a clearing, with the river on your right. You are now in a mixed landscape of long grass and thinly-spaced birch trees. This is one of several spots on the route where you have a chance of seeing deer. In spring and summer, it is also a particularly good place to see butterflies.

The footpath follows the river as it loops around the edge of the clearing. Away to your left, the land rises steeply and is thickly covered with trees. As you progress, the trees close in from the left and the path becomes sandy.

5.   After 300 m, you arrive at the edge of a small copse. Here there is a boardwalk, a welcome enhancement to the route that makes it accessible all year round. Without it, the path is impossibly boggy and not nearly as enjoyable.

Get Home Quicker ▶ Turn around at this point and retrace your steps to town if you would like to keep your walk under 1 hour. Otherwise, continue on as described below.

At the end of the boardwalk, keep straight for 20 m to emerge from the trees into a large field. Turn right and follow the path along the tree line at the edge of this field. The river is on your right beyond the trees. In spring, there are bluebells here, and in autumn, lots of chestnuts.

6.   When you reach the corner of the field, the path descends down a short slope and into a second field. The river is now close by on your right, but only briefly. It quickly moves away again and is only just visible through the trees as you continue to make your way along the edge of the field.

7.   At the far corner of the second field, there is a gate that takes you into Woolbeding Parkland. The path now strikes a diagonal line across the grass and up towards a small wood. This area is often used to graze cattle or sheep, so it's important to keep dogs on a lead.

See More River ▶ To stay with the river, ignore the grass track heading up the hill and continue to follow the fence on your right until you come to a gate. Pass through the gate to follow a faint path across uneven ground towards a small lake. Keeping the river on your right and the lake on your left, continue to follow the path until you come to another gate. Go through into a large field, which is on the other side of the hill that you saw at Point **7.** By following the river, you have skirted around the hill rather than going over it. Head up a steep slope to join the wide track that runs down the centre of the field. Turn right onto it, heading down towards a fence and five-bar gate. Now skip ahead to Point **9.**

As you make your way up the hill, keep an eye out for Woolbeding House. It is away to your right and very well obscured by trees. Owned by the National Trust but privately rented, its gardens are open on specific days during the summer for pre-booked visits. As you reach the gate at the top of the field, you may also catch a glimpse of the tiny All Hallows Church to the left of the house.

A new feature to look out for is the Woolbeding Glasshouse. Designed by Heatherwick Studios, it is a glass structure rather like an upturned diamond. In summer, the upper sections open like a lily to provide ventilation for the plants inside.

8.   At the top of the slope, go through the gate and into a small wood. Here, the path is wide, cool, and shady. A welcome respite on a hot day. The trees are old and impressively tall as they tower above you.

VIEWS WORTH WALKING FOR

The wood is dense, and as you emerge on the other side, the sweeping views to the left and right will surprise and delight you. The river is once again visible as it makes its way to Woolbeding Bridge, and the pine trees of Severals Pine Forest rise up ahead of you. Looking slightly to the right, you can see the striking outline of Beacon Hill on the South Downs Way.

9.   Follow the wide track all the way to the far side of this large field. Pass through the gate and, unless you are intending to explore Midhurst Common (see variation below), ignore the signpost that tells you that the Rother Walk is straight on. Instead, follow the path to your left, and after 100 m, go through a gate into a small field.

Stay Out Longer   ▶   If you would like to explore Midhurst Common, carry straight on to pass through a gate and into a small car park. Exit the car park onto a lane. Turn left onto the lane to meet the A272. Cross the A272 and follow a track into the woodland. Continuing straight on this track will bring you to Severals Road. Turning onto any footpath on your left will take you further into the woodland and across the Common.

In the middle of the wood is a large clearing. To the north of this clearing there is a steep hill (Sunset Hill) with great views towards the South Downs. To exit the Common, take any path towards Bepton Road or Carron Lane. The sketch map will help you but if you are not familiar with the Common, you are advised to use a digital map to track your route.

WALK ONE - EXTENSION MAP
Midhurst Common

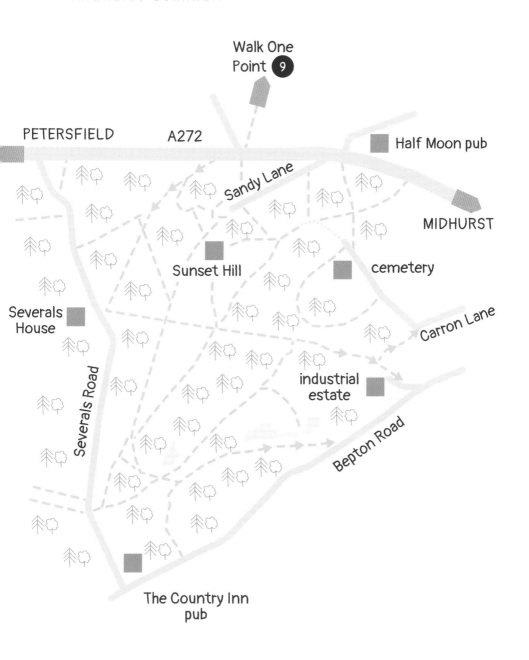

Walk One
Point **9**

PETERSFIELD A272 Half Moon pub

Sandy Lane

MIDHURST

Sunset Hill

cemetery

Severals
House

Carron Lane

Severals Road

industrial
estate

Bepton Road

The Country Inn
pub

10. Continue to the far side of this field, where the path goes over a culvert. To your right is a wooden bridge. Ahead of you and slightly left is an unmarked path leading down a grassy slope to meet a dirt track. This will bring you out onto June Lane just opposite the Half Moon pub. Take this path, and when you get to June Lane, turn left to follow it up the hill.

11. Just as you reach the peak of the hill, there is a small parking area to your left. As June Lane heads down again towards the town, there is no pavement. Take care as you walk along the road, making sure you can easily see any oncoming traffic.

Get Home Quicker ▶ If you prefer to go straight back to town at this point, stay on June Lane. After 700 m, you will arrive at a T-junction. Turn left onto North Street and cross at the first pedestrian crossing. Turn right to walk back up North Street to the junction with Knockhundred Row. Turn left and follow the road up and round to the right to arrive back at Market Square.

A SMALLHOLDING WITH BIG VIEWS

After 100 m, you come to a five-bar gate and a stone wall. There is a gap in the wall with steps leading up to another, smaller gate. Go through this gate to follow a footpath around the edge of stables and fields belonging to a small farm. This path is initially quite narrow and can be muddy, but after a steep descent, it widens out into the fields below.

12. As you get to the bottom of the slope, the path turns sharply to the right along the edge of a field, which rises steeply to your left. The path here is sandy and suffers erosion from the water that runs off the hill. As a result, the track can be very uneven, and remediation work is sometimes needed to maintain the land around the edge of this field.

Ahead of you are the buildings of Midhurst Rother College. As you reach the boundary fence, the path turns sharply to the left and leads you into a small copse. Bear right as soon as you enter the copse, to stay close to the boundary of the school.

13.   The path heads up a slight slope and then down again but always keeping you close to the school fence. You are on the edge of woodland which, in spring, has a sprinkling of bluebells. The path levels out as it turns to the right and continues to follow the fence. After 100 m, turn left, away from the school, heading down a gentle slope to join the path you were on at the start of the walk.

14.   Turn right at the T-junction, keeping the river to your left. The weir is ahead and after 150 m, you emerge from the woods beside the main road again. Cowdray Ruins are on the far side of the fields in front of you.

Turn right and retrace your steps back past the entrance to Midhurst Rother College, the Methodist Church, and South Downs Centre. From here, cross the road at the pedestrian crossing to walk back up North Street. Turn left to walk along Knockhundred Row and Church Hill back to Market Square.

ICE CREAM AND DOGS: WHAT'S NOT TO LOVE AT FITZCANE'S CAFÉ?

Today, you will find Fitzcane's Café on North Street, just a stone's throw from the car park and bus station. Scroll back to 2014 and you would have found a much smaller version of it on Grange Road in a quirky little building that used to be a diner and is now a clock shop.

In those early days, it was a bit of a mystery how owner, Caroline Cheshire, managed to deliver such an array of tasty offerings from such a small kitchen or how she managed to make all of her customers (two-legged and four-legged) feel they were part of one big happy family. With plenty of games to keep children amused, special treats for dogs, and ice cream as a central theme, the fledgling Fitzcane's was a huge hit with locals and visitors alike.

BIGGER SHOP, MORE ICE CREAM

Moving to larger premises in North Street gave Caroline an opportunity to expand her unique café style and her warm welcome. In comfortable and colourful surroundings, you can enjoy breakfast, lunch, or afternoon tea, all made from fresh, locally sourced ingredients. As you'd expect from a café where everyone is always welcome, there are plenty of vegetarian, vegan, and gluten free options on the menu.

"I want friends to enjoy eating out together whatever their dietary requirements." says Caroline.

Fitzcane's takes great pride in their ethically sourced coffee, so you'll get free filter coffee refills as part of the service. This is just one of the ideas that Caroline brought with from her time spent living in Boston, USA. Bagels, homemade waffles, and the idea you could go out just to eat dessert are others.

As a responsible café, Fitzcane's is also committed to using recycled and compostable cups and packaging. They also provide free tap water as part of the 'water-on-the-go' campaign.

On sunny days, enjoy your visit in the pretty garden, but you won't be forced to sit there if you've arrived with your dog. Just like everyone else, dogs are welcomed at Fitzcane's, indoors or out. They get free treats and there is even dog-friendly ice cream on the menu.

Wrap up your visit by treating yourself to one of the many Midhurst-related gifts on offer. Thoughtfully selected and inventively displayed, they include mugs, cushions, and other inexpensive reminders of your visit to this quirky and inviting café.

WALK TWO / ➡ 9 km / ⏳ 3 hours

Or three separate walks of ➡ 3 km / ⏳ 1 hour

THE ONE WITH THE CASTLE, THE RUIN, AND ROYAL CONNECTIONS

This is a walk that anyone with an interest in Medieval and Tudor history will enjoy. Midhurst was an important market town from as early as the 12th century and has over 100 listed buildings.

The Town Trail is a good supplement to this walk. You should be able to get a copy from the South Downs Centre on North Street. If you would like to know more about the history of the town, The Midhurst Society and Wheeler's Bookshop are both useful sources of information.

From the start point at Market Square, it is a short stroll to St. Ann's Hill and the remains of Midhurst Castle. Whilst all you can see today are the foundations of the 12th century fortified manor house, the history of the site goes back much further, with evidence of a motte-and-bailey castle and an Iron Age fort all on this one spot. Rising high above the river, it is easy to see why the location was chosen, and it is captivating to imagine what it might have been like to live there.

Descending a steep flight of steps, you follow a path along the river to Cowdray Ruins. This is all that remains of what was a rather splendid Tudor house that played host to King Henry VIII, Elizabeth I, and possibly also Edward VI.

Its present condition is almost entirely the result of a fire that broke out in 1793, after which it was never inhabited again. In 2006, conservation work was carried out, making it possible to open it up to visitors and for events.

The route continues to Easebourne village, the Cowdray Park Golf Course, and the Queen Elizabeth Oak. Along the way, look out for polo matches, which are played throughout the summer months. The name of Cowdray has long been associated with polo, and several members of the current royal family have played here.

A VERY SPECIAL TREE

The Queen Elizabeth Oak is found on the far side of the golf course. It is a special tree, and not just because it is well over 800 years old. By girth, it is the third largest oak tree on record in the UK, and it is said that Elizabeth I once sheltered under its branches. Since 2002, it has been officially dedicated to both Elizabeth I and Elizabeth II. It is one of fifty 'Great British Trees', designated in recognition of its place in our national heritage.

The tree theme continues with a walk along an avenue of limes. These were planted in 2012 to commemorate the diamond jubilee of Queen Elizabeth II. You are then well set to explore the John Cowdray Arboretum, after visiting Benbow Pond, which is home to several unusual, and rather striking, black swans.

The return journey to Midhurst provides excellent views towards the South Downs, Cowdray Ruins, and the town itself, nestling among its wooded hills. If you are nervous of walking on the golf course, there are variations below that enable visits to Easebourne and the Queen Elizabeth Oak without including the golf course.

THE ONE WITH THE CASTLE, THE RUIN, AND ROYAL CONNECTIONS

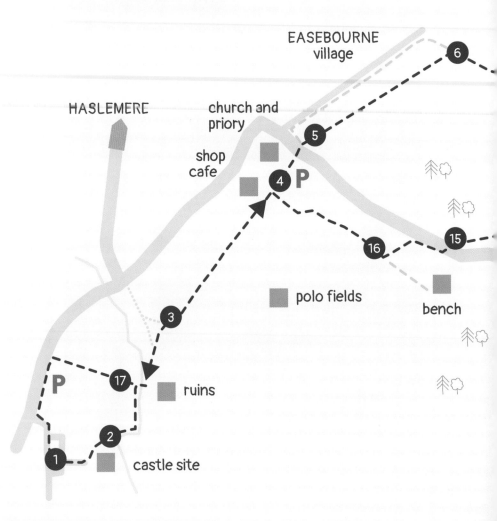

EASEBOURNE
village

HASLEMERE

church and
priory

shop
cafe

P

polo fields

bench

ruins

castle site

1	route guide		walk route
	woods		alternative route
	site of interest		footpath/track
P	parking		road

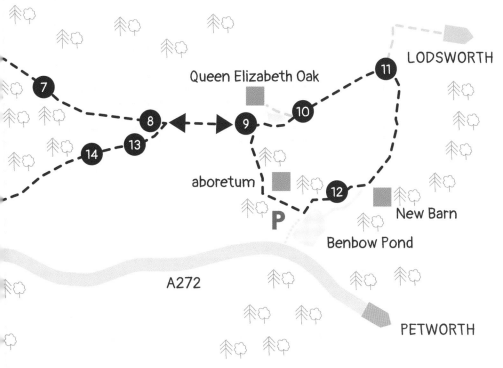

LODSWORTH

Queen Elizabeth Oak

aboretum

New Barn

Benbow Pond

A272

PETWORTH

➲ VARIATIONS

If you complete it as written, this walk will take 3 hours. It is possible to reduce it by 30–40 minutes if you turn back at Stewards Pond and pick up the return route from Point **13.** This variation misses out the avenue of Limes, Benbow Pond, and the arboretum.

THREE SHORT WALKS

Another option is to split the walk into three sections: Midhurst, Easebourne, and Benbow Pond. By splitting the walk in this way, you can miss out the golf course and create routes that can each be completed in around 1 hour. Sketch maps are provided at the end of the chapter to show each of these short walks in more detail.

If you prefer a longer walk, you can extend the route in various ways on either side of the A272. A recommended option is to head to Lodsworth. This pretty village has a general store, as well as a pub and tearoom. The shop was designed and built by Ben Law, a woodsman whose house-build featured in an episode of Grand Designs. The shop is built using the same technique that Ben used for his house and is well worth a visit, as much for the building as for its local produce.

REALLY LONG AND LINEAR

After visiting Lodsworth, you can retrace your steps to complete the route as written or head further east to the villages of River, Upperton, and Tillington. This extension takes you through some beautiful countryside, but you may not want to make this a circular route. Options for getting back to Midhurst include hopping on one of the regular bus services, organising your own transport, or simply retracing your steps.

If you do want to make this a full day-hike, you can find footpaths from Tillington that will take you across the A272 and onto farmland that stretches almost all the way to the foot of the Downs.

You can make your way back to Midhurst without needing to go quite as far as the Downs by crossing Duncton, Lavington, Graffham, and Heyshott Commons. An OS Explorer map is recommended, and arguably essential, if you want to explore this far afield.

➲ AMENITIES

As well as a variety of pubs, cafés, and shops in Midhurst, you will pass the Cowdray Farm Shop & Café as you reach Easebourne. If you extend the walk all the way to Tillington, you have café and pub options in both Lodsworth and Tillington. There is also a pub in Easebourne called The White Horse. It can be found just a short way along Easebourne Street, just off the A272, opposite the church.

If you decide on a full day-hike, you would do well to go via Heath End, where there is a pub, farm shop, and café. Also at Heath End is an unusual B&B called The Old Railway Station. As the name suggests, it used to be a station, and, delightfully, a number of its guest rooms are converted Pullman carriages. Afternoon tea is available in the beautifully restored waiting room. You don't need to be a guest to visit the tearoom, but you do need to book in advance. It is well worth a visit whether you include it in your walking route or not.

➲ ROUTE GUIDE

1. Make your way across Market Square, away from the Swan Inn, with the church on your left and Garton's Coffee House on your right. Be sure to look at the stocks recessed into the side wall of the coffee house. This building used to be the Town Hall and Fire Station.

Behind the coffee house is St. Ann's Hill, a short road that ends at a five-bar gate. Go through the gate to enter the castle site, where you can freely explore the foundations of the fortified manor. There are several footpaths encircling the hilltop. To continue the walk, take the path on the left from the gate, following it around the hill with the castle remains on your right. After 100 m, head down a set of steep wooden steps to the river.

2. When you reach the bottom of the steps, continue ahead through a gate. Keeping the river on your right, follow the path as it curves around to the left. After 200 m, you arrive at a stone bridge, and a wide track stretching away to your left. Cross the bridge.

TAKE TEA AT THE RUINS

You are now facing Cowdray Ruins, and if you have organised a visit, turn right to find the entrance to the Cowdray Heritage Trust. Alongside the Trust is the entrance to 'The Walled Garden'. This is primarily an event venue but it is occasionally open to the public. In summer, it is often possible to book ahead for afternoon tea in the garden tearoom.

Get Home Quicker ▶ If you would like to split this walk into 3 sections (Midhurst, Easebourne, and Benbow Pond), you can turn around here and retrace your steps back to Market Square. Alternatively, you can follow the wide track across the fields in front of the ruins. This will bring you out at the North Street Car Park. From here, make your way onto North Street and turn left, passing shops and cafés until you reach Knockhundred Row. Turn left into this road and follow it round to the right into Church Hill and Market Square. A third option is to follow the route guide as far as Point **4.** This enables you to visit Cowdray Farm Shop & Café before heading back to the start point. The walk from Cowdray Ruins to the Farm Shop and Café takes around 15 minutes each way.

To continue the walk, turn left in front of the ruins to follow a boundary fence along the access road ahead. As the access road bears left around a triangular green, continue straight, on a rough track, remaining close to the boundary fence. Pass cricket nets and a small parking area to arrive at a double five-bar gate.

3.   Pass through a gap to the left of the gate to follow a wide dirt track that runs along the edge of polo fields. Take care as this track is sometimes used by vehicles making their way to the parking areas for large events and polo matches. If there is a polo match in progress, it is fun to stop and watch. Many matches are free for spectators, and the atmosphere is often competitive and exciting. You don't need to understand how to play to enjoy the spectacle!

4.   Follow the track for 700 m, making your way around another double five-bar gate at the far end. As you near the gate, the path becomes a metalled track, and Cowdray Farm Shop & Café are ahead on the left. On the right, note the grassed picnic area. You will see this again as you emerge from fields at the end of the walk (Point **16.**). Keep straight past the café and shop.

Stay on the metalled track to pass in front of Easebourne Priory. This attractive building was established as a priory in the 13th century and closed in 1535 when it was converted into a private residence. Queen Elizabeth I was a guest here during her visit to Cowdray in 1591.

Attached to the Priory is The Parish Church of St. Mary, which dates back as far the 11th Century. One of its four bells is thought to have come from a chapel on the site of the fortified manor house that you visited earlier, on St. Ann's Hill.

Get Home Quicker   ▶   If you are splitting the walk into three separate sections, the parking area opposite the farm shop, café, and church is the best place to start the second section. You can make a short circular walk by following Point **5.** until you get to the footpath crossroads. Turn left, instead of right, to emerge onto Easebourne Street. Turn left again to follow this road through the village and back to the junction with the A272. Another option is to follow the route guide for Points **15.** and **16.** from the picnic tables and out into the fields beyond. Walking at first between two wooden fences and then across an open field, you will arrive at a gate and a second field. Heading straight across this field brings you to a small pond. The pond itself is very overgrown but there are two wooden benches to the left of it. Sitting here, you can admire the views across the polo fields to the ruins, the town, and the South Downs.

5.   To continue the main route, head to the T-junction with the A272. Directly opposite is the entrance to a wide, tree-lined path. Cross the road, pass through two gates, and follow the path for 750 m until you get to a footpath crossroad.

This path is known as 'The Race' and is an avenue of ancient sweet chestnut trees. It can be muddy in winter or after heavy rainfall. To the right there is a field, and intermittently visible on the left are the cottages of Easebourne village. The footpath crossroad is clearly marked with a fingerpost. When you get to it, turn right to cut across the long narrow field that you have been walking alongside. If you are opting for a shorter route, turn left here to cut through to Easebourne Street and follow the variation above.

6. On the far side of the field, there is a gate. Go through it and up a short slope onto the Cowdray Park Golf Course. Make your way across the fairway and down towards a small copse.

TAKE CARE ON THE GOLF COURSE

Ensure that, while you are on the golf course, you keep to the marked footpaths. Take special care whenever you need to cross the line of play. The footpaths are not always easy to see, but there are fingerposts to guide you. Golfers are used to seeing walkers on the footpaths and will help you if you lose your way.

7. The path descends along the edge of the copse until it arrives at the 4th Tee. Bear left at the fork to head up again and out onto a fairway. When you reach the fairway, head across it, bearing slightly left towards a footpath sign. From this sign, head straight and then cross another fairway into an area of rough grass.

Follow a path across the grass and over a third fairway. Head straight as you leave the fairway, to enter another copse and pick up a narrow footpath. In spring, this copse is full of bluebells. In summer, it can get overgrown with bracken, so the footpath is not always clear.

8. After 100 m, a fingerpost marks the point where a path joins from the right. This is the path you will take on your return journey after seeing the Queen Elizabeth Oak, Benbow Pond, and the Arboretum. It also marks the point where you leave the golf course for a while. Keep ahead for another 200 m until you see a wooden gate on your left.

9. Through this gate, and somewhat hidden behind brambles and small trees, is Stewards Pond. Bear right to make your way around the pond in an anticlockwise direction until you see an avenue of young lime trees. These are easily identified by the wooden deer protection around the lower trunks. The route continues along this avenue, but to see the Queen Elizabeth Oak, make your way a little further around the pond.

WHICH ONE IS IT?

Look for a tree that has a short but very wide trunk that is almost completely hollow. Behind the Elizabeth Oak is a second very similar oak tree, known as the Lady in Waiting. Both are usually protected by fencing. The Queen Elizabeth Oak has a small commemorative sign in front of it.

10. Once you have seen the Queen Elizabeth Oak, you may choose to shorten the walk by retracing your steps back to the gate and along the track to find the path noted in Point **8.** If you want to do this, pick up the route guide again at Point **13.** Otherwise, make your way through the avenue of lime trees to the far corner of the field, where there is a gate. From this gate, you can extend the walk to Lodsworth by following the variation below.

Stay Out Longer ▶ If you plan to extend this walk to Lodsworth or beyond, turn left after passing through the gate and follow the footpath around the edge of the field. There is a gate at the far corner of this field. Pass through and follow a footpath along the edge of a wood until you arrive at a country lane. Keep straight to follow the lane for 400 m until you come to a fork. You are now at the edge of Lodsworth village. Bear right to follow another road down to a T-junction. When you reach the T-junction, turn left to find the village shop and tearoom on your left behind the pub. Make sure you have access to an OS map if you plan to extend your walk further to River, Upperton, and Tillington.

11. To continue the main route, pass through the gate and turn right. Follow the edge of the field towards Benbow Pond and a residence called New Barn. After 400 m, you draw level with New Barn and the path descends quite steeply towards a five-bar gate. When you reach the gate, follow the fence line to the right until a gap in the fence allows you to access the parking area beside Benbow Pond.

12. Head straight, along the access road, keeping the pond on your left. Look for a sign on the right welcoming you to the John Cowdray Arboretum. Pass through the gap in the low wooden fence to take the right-hand grass pathway up through the trees.

IS THIS WHERE THE FAIRIES MEET?

After 80 m, you see five grass paths ahead. Take the third path from the left to keep straight. As you pass by, note the wooden furniture on the left, just right for little people. After another 100 m, you come to the edge of the golf course, and the path bends away to the right. Follow it down a slope to reach a T-junction. Directly ahead, you will see the avenue of limes. Turn left at the junction, and after 70 m, you arrive again, at the gate that leads to Stewards Pond.

Get Home Quicker ▶ If you are starting your walk at Benbow Pond, follow the route as described for Point **12**. This will take you through the arboretum to the gate that leads to Stewards Pond. Then follow the route description given in Point **9.** to find the Queen Elizabeth Oak. You could retrace your steps back through the arboretum or use Points **10.** and **11.** in the route guide to head through the avenue of limes and back to Benbow Pond via the field behind New Barn. This circular route takes less than 1 hour to complete.

13. After 200 m, you come to the fork noted at Point **8.** Keep left to climb the slope until you emerge from the trees onto a fairway. Weather permitting, you will now have extraordinarily good views of the South Downs, all the way back into Midhurst.

14. Bear right to pass between the two wooden huts ahead of you. Bear right again to keep Tee 15 on your left. Cross a metalled path and look left for a fingerpost beside a large chestnut tree. Head from this fingerpost straight along the edge of the fairway, with rough grass on your right and the fairway itself on your left.

As you make your way along, look out for an old oak tree that has bent so far over that its branches touch the ground. The path gradually descends until you see three bunkers ahead. Pass between the first two bunkers and keep left to follow the footpath towards the road ahead.

15. When you come to the road, turn right. After 20 m, cross carefully to walk along a wide verge, with the road on your right. After 100 m, there is a gate on the left. Pass through the gate into a field. Turn to your right to walk around the edge of the field in an anticlockwise direction.

TAKE A SEAT

Walk all the way along the first side of the field and turn left to continue along the second side. Halfway along this second side is a gate. As you reach the gate, look to your left, towards the middle of the field. Beside a solitary tree and a collection of brambles, there are two wooden benches with good views towards Cowdray Ruins and the South Downs. They make a good diversion if you would like to stop and rest at this point.

16. To continue, pass through the gate and make your way across a second field towards another gate. Beyond this, there is a wooden fence on either side of the path. After 50 m, the path opens out into the picnic area noted at Point **4.**

Cross the picnic area to reach the wide track that leads to Cowdray Farm Shop & Café. Turn left onto the track (away from the shop and café) to retrace your steps past the polo fields, and back to Cowdray Ruins.

17. As you arrive at Cowdray Ruins, you have a choice. You can retrace your steps back to the castle site and go from there to Market Square. Alternatively, you can walk down the causeway to arrive in Midhurst via the North Street Car Park. If you choose the latter option, make your way along North Street until you reach Knockhundred Row on your left. Follow this road around to the right as it becomes Church Hill. Just past the church, you will find Market Square where you started the walk.

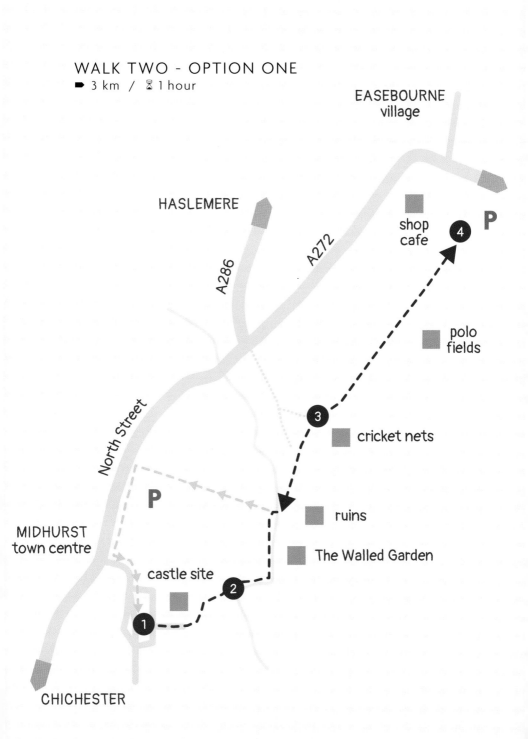

WALK TWO - OPTION ONE
➡ 3 km / ⌛ 1 hour

EASEBOURNE
village

HASLEMERE

A286

A272

North street

shop
cafe

P

polo
fields

cricket nets

P

ruins

The Walled Garden

MIDHURST
town centre

castle site

CHICHESTER

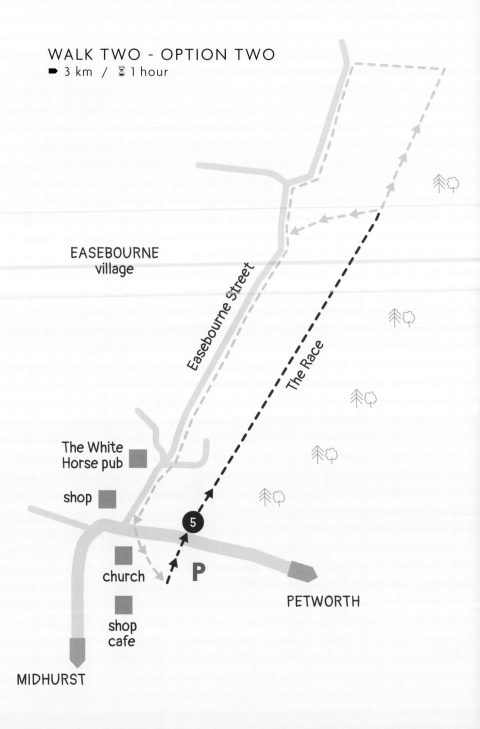

WALK TWO - OPTION TWO
➡ 3 km / ⏳ 1 hour

EASEBOURNE
village

Easebourne Street

The Race

The White
Horse pub

shop

church

P

5

PETWORTH

shop
cafe

MIDHURST

WALK TWO - OPTION THREE
➡ 3 km / ⧗ 1 hour

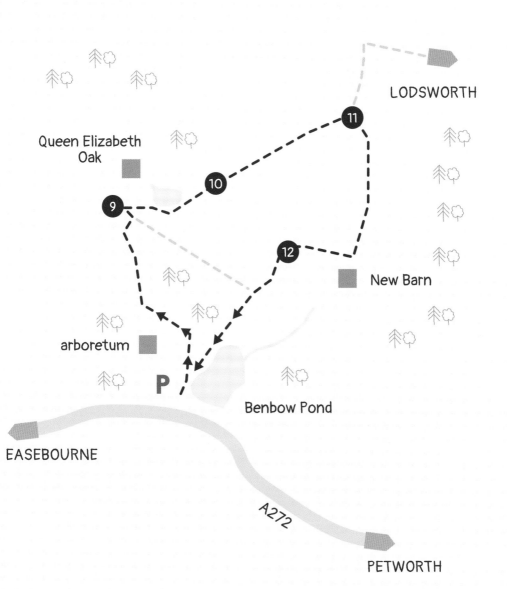

COMESTIBLES DELICATESSEN & CAFÉ

You will find Comestibles just opposite Market Square on Red Lion Street. It is primarily a delicatessen and takeaway sandwich shop, but it has a small seating area inside, and, in dry weather, you'll find several tables outside too. If you want to sit and watch Midhurst go about its business while you have breakfast, lunch, or a fantastic cup of coffee (made with organic milk from Goodwood), this is the place to go.

The shop is in one of the oldest parts of town, and the building itself dates back to the 17th century. It used to be a pub (The Red Lion), but there has been a delicatessen called Comestibles on the premises for as long as most locals can remember. Owner Brendon Davies took over back in 2005, making quite a significant career change to go into business with his sister.

From the outset, the goal was to provide great food and great value. Almost two decades later, this winning combination is still going strong, with a loyal following of local customers, as well as visitors, who are delighted to discover this unique, independent business in the heart of the old town.

Almost everything on the menu is made from scratch on the premises. Quiches are a popular speciality, and it's not unusual to find three or four different types on offer. More recently, the Comestibles team have branched out into what they call 'ready meals'. Homemade sweet and savoury pies, crumbles, and pasta dishes literally fly out of the door, all ready to be heated up at home and devoured.

A delight at any time of year, Comestibles really does come into its own at Christmas. Beautifully packaged, food-based gifts line the shelves, and the jingle of the bell above the door gives the whole store a wonderfully Dickensian Yuletide feel. Nothing quite beats heading inside for a steaming cup of hot chocolate, some last-minute gifts, and maybe a mince pie or two.

Of course, it is the staff that truly makes Comestibles an all-round delight. You would be hard pushed to find a nicer bunch. Friendly and welcoming, these are people who are more disappointed than you if they have sold out of the very item you came in for. Phone ahead to place an order if you're popping in for takeaway, or, better still, sit in the sun at the outside tables and relax while the Comestibles team look after you.

THE ONE WITH THE COMMONS

You will spend almost all your time on this walk on common land that has, over many years, grown into beautiful mixed wood and heathland. The majority of the trees are pine, but there are also silver birch, chestnut, and oak trees. It is a haven for wildlife, with birds, butterflies, and deer all relatively easy to spot.

The first part of the route takes you through Midhurst Common before continuing into Severals Pine Forest and crossing the nature reserve on Stedham Common. As you pass through the nature reserve, you are on heathland that is both rare and remarkable.

RARE AND BEAUTIFUL

You are on one of several small pockets of lowland heath that are spread across the Western Weald, home to a variety of insects and reptiles and one of the only habitats that can support the relatively rare Dartford Warbler. In summer, native heather comes into flower, turning the landscape into stunning shades of purple and lilac.

WITH STUNNING VIEWS

After exiting the heath, you will be treated to beautiful views of the South Downs as you pass through Mitchell's Common, and cross farmland towards Minsted. Crossing a tributary of the River Rother, you will find yourself in another striking pine forest called The Warren. On the edge of Bepton village, you re-enter Midhurst Common to make your way back to the start point.

WALK THREE
➡ 10 km / ⌛ 3¼ hours

THE ONE WITH THE COMMONS

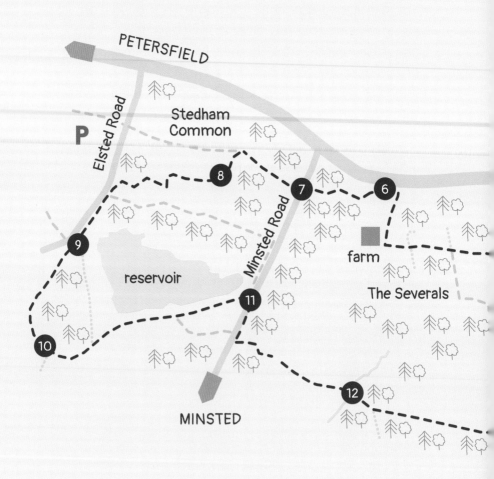

Symbol	Meaning	Symbol	Meaning
1 route guide		walk route	
woods		alternative route	
site of interest		footpath/track	
P parking		road	

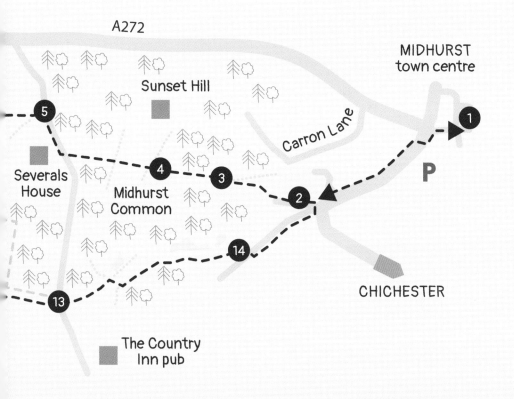

A272

MIDHURST town centre

Sunset Hill

Carron Lane

5

Severals House

4

3

2

1

P

Midhurst Common

14

CHICHESTER

13

The Country Inn pub

⮌ VARIATIONS

It is possible to make very enjoyable shorter loops within the overall route for this walk. The first and shortest option guides you through Severals Pine Forest to re-join the main route at Point **13**. This variation takes 1½ hours to complete. The second variation misses out the Fitzhall section of the route to make a loop around Stedham Common and takes 2½ hours to complete.

There is parking at Iping Common, and you could use it to explore the nature reserves and commons without walking from Midhurst. You will find this small car park just off the Elsted Road. It is shown on the route map and is only a short drive along the A272 from Midhurst. If you choose to do this, you can mix and match trails from the suggested route and the extension to create a route of your own choosing.

To extend the route, you can continue through Stedham Common into Iping and Trotton Commons. There are several trails across these two commons, and you can re-join the main route via the Fitzhall Plantation. An additional sketch map is provided to help you navigate this extension.

⮌ AMENITIES

There are cafés and pubs in Midhurst but no other amenities on the walk itself. If you take slight detour as you arrive at Bepton, near the end of the walk, you could stop at The Country Inn.

⮌ ROUTE GUIDE

1. With your back to Garton's Coffee House, cross Church Hill and bear left around The Swan Inn onto West Street. Follow West Street to the mini roundabout at its far end and turn left onto Bepton Road. Cross over Bepton Road at the pedestrian crossing and turn again to your left. Continue along the pavement for 600 m until you come to a sharp bend with a T-junction at its apex. Somewhat confusingly, the turning off the main road is a continuation of Bepton Road. As the main road makes the sharp bend to the left, it becomes New Road.

2. Turn onto Bepton Road and immediately bear right onto Station Road. After 70 m, take the footpath on your right and then bear left at a fork onto a path that runs along the edge of the woodland. The buildings of an industrial estate are visible just the other side of a fence on your left. Continue for 300 m until the path rises steeply to join a wide track with telephone wires overhead.

3. Turn left onto this track, following its overhead wires for 200 m until it merges with another track on your right. Keep straight, with the telephone wires overhead, until you arrive at a clearing. Away to the right, the land rises up to Sunset Hill. From the top of this hill, there are beautiful views across to the South Downs. You could make a detour now or visit it as part of the route on Walk Four.

4. Keep straight across the clearing and head into the woods on the opposite side. With the telephone wires remaining overhead, continue for 150 m, to arrive at a metal gate and a road. This is Severals Road, and directly opposite there is a property called Severals House. Pass through the gap to the left of the gate and turn right to walk along the road.

5. Continue on Severals Road for 200 m. As the road bends to the left, there is a well-hidden footpath on the left (to ensure you are in the right place, look for a metal gate on the right). Turn left onto the path, which is narrow at first but quickly widens and then splits into three. Take the path farthest to the right and then bear right again at a fork. Keep straight on this path for 300 m until you reach a footpath crossroads.

If you want to keep your walk short, turn left and follow the variation notes below. Otherwise, head straight across and follow the path as it descends steadily and turns to the right. After 50 m, there is a T-junction. Turn right to continue, along the side of the hill. Away to your left, farm buildings are visible through the trees. The path ends at a metalled access road, where you turn left to cross a stone bridge.

Get Home Quicker ▶ Turning left at the footpath crossroad, you find yourself on a straight path that descends gradually. After 200 m, turn left at another footpath crossroad. Bear right at the next fork and follow the path as it curves gently to the left and then to the right. A large square clearing opens up on your right. This area was cleared as part of ongoing forest management, so over time it will re-grow. Walk along one whole side of the cleared area and then turn right at the footpath crossroad to walk along the whole of the adjacent side. Turn left when you reach the T-junction at the end of the second side of the clearing. Continue straight until you arrive at Severals Road. Turn right onto the road and then left, to cross the parking area and re-join the main route at Point **13.**

6. Ahead is the entrance to a farm. To the right of its driveway there is a footpath. Take this path, and follow it along the boundary fence for 70 m, to arrive at a fork. Bear right to head up a steady incline on a woodland path. Continue straight for 300 m until you come to a road. This is Minsted Road, and opposite is a gate leading to Stedham Common Nature Reserve.

7. Go through the gate and follow the path straight ahead for 300 m to reach a sandstone bench on your right. A sculpture as well as a seat, it is called 'Dragonflies Rest' and is one of seven sculptures on lowland heath sites across the South Downs National Park.

WALK THREE - EXTENSION MAP
Iping Common

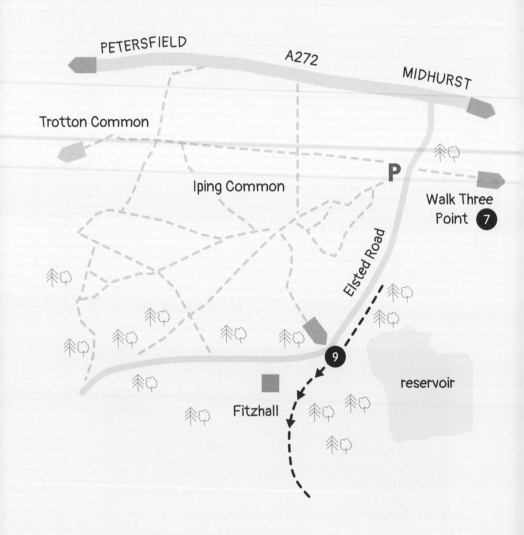

The sculpture seat is situated near a slightly offset footpath crossroad, and the main route continues along a turning to the left some 10 m away. If you want to extend your walk onto Iping Common, follow the notes below. Otherwise, take the turning on the left to make your way down a gentle slope.

Stay Out Longer ▶ Keep straight until you reach the Elsted Road. You will then be able to follow the routes on the extension map (left) to make your own way across Iping and Trotton commons and back to join the main route at Point **9.** via Fitzhall Plantation.

After 80 m, there is a hollow where a rope swing hangs from one of the surrounding trees. Take a footpath on the right, just beyond this hollow. Keep straight as a path joins from the left and then bear left at a fork 50 m ahead.

HELP THE SUSSEX WILDLIFE TRUST

Off the route, away to your right, is a thick wooden post with a metal frame on top of it. This is a 'photo post'. Use the metal frame to support your smartphone and share your photo on social media with the hashtag **#SWTPhotoPosts**. By doing this you are providing the Sussex Wildlife Trust with a photographic record of how the landscape changes over time.

8. Keep straight for 130 m, until you come to a fork. Bear left to remain on the wide track as it bends to the left, then to the right. After 70 m turn left at a T-junction. A final right-hand bend brings you to fingerpost. Ahead there is a five bar gate leading to the road.

With the fingerpost immediately on your right, turn left to pass through a wooden gate and exit the nature reserve. Keep straight for 250 m, on this path, parallel to the road. If you prefer to shorten the walk at this point, look for a path on the left 30 m after passing through the gate and follow the variation notes below.

Get Home Quicker ▶ Take the left turn to follow a footpath through the woods on the edge of the common. This side of the common is quite boggy, which provides a wonderful habitat for dragonflies. Keep straight for 600 m, until you come to Minsted Road. Exit the common via a wooden gate and turn right onto Minsted Road. Follow it for 450 m before turning left onto a wide track to re-join the main route at Point **11.**

9. Continuing the main route, keep straight until you come to a footpath crossroad. Go straight across and 40 m further along there is a second crossroad. Looking to the right you see the Elsted Road. There is a five bar gate on the opposite side and this is where the extension re-joins the main route, from Iping Common.

Go straight across the crossroad onto a path that has large rhododendron bushes on both sides. After 30 m, there is a pine tree glade on the left. Continue straight, with the glade on your left and the driveway to Fitzhall (a Grade II listed private residence) on your right.

A VIEW TO THE DOWNS

After 180 m, cross a track to head down to a T-junction. Turn left onto a metalled road. This is the access road to Fitzhall Cottage. It passes through a deep-sided cutting before bending to the left at the driveway to the cottage itself. Continue past the cottage, bearing left at a fork, to follow a path between two fields. As this path curves to the left, there are stunning views towards the South Downs on your right.

10. Head towards a wood, where two thick round posts on either side of the path mark its boundary. Enter the wood, and after 70 m, bear right at a fork to follow a wide dirt track that has a fence on the left. This fence separates the path from a large reservoir. Take note of the warning signs and stay away from the water. It is deep, and the sides of the reservoir are steep.

MUD, GLORIOUS MUD

Keep straight on the footpath as it descends gently and becomes narrower. At almost any time of year this path can be boggy, particularly the section through the trees. As the path emerges from the wood there is a field on the right and views towards the South Downs. After 350 m, there is a fork, and you can take either path.

Heading straight, on the wide, tree-lined track is usually a less muddy option, but you will have to walk on the Minsted Road for longer. Bearing right can lead you to some large, deep puddles or flood water if the weather has been particularly wet. If you choose this path, it makes a sharp bend to the left after 50 m, to pass in front of a small row of cottages before bringing you out to the Minsted Road.

11. At the road, turn right and walk along it for 75–200 m, depending on which path you chose above. Here is where the second, shorter variation re-joins the main route. Turn left onto a wide track and follow it round to the left, then right, and left again to pass in front of two cottages. The first cottage has an old shepherd's hut parked in front of it, and there are often pygmy goats in the small field opposite.

Ahead, two fields meet. The gates to these fields are sometimes closed and sometimes open, so navigate around them to walk along the edge of the right-hand field, with the fence on your left. The South Downs run parallel to this path, so there are good views across the fields on your right. When you reach the far side of the field, go through a metal gate and straight across a small area of rough ground. Taking a straight line across the grass, you come to another metal gate and a concrete bridge over a stream.

12. Go through the gate and across the stream to follow the path up a short slope into the pine tree wood known as 'The Warren'. Bear left at the fork to follow a straight path through the woods. After 500 m, the footpath turns into a brick path. The bricks are white and were almost certainly made at the Midhurst Brickworks, which closed in 1985.

After another 200 m, the path brings you out onto a metalled road beside Oakwood House. Turn left and almost immediately cross Severals Road. At this point, you are on the edge of Bepton village, and should you wish to make a detour, the Country Inn is 300 m along the road, to your right.

13. To continue the main route, head across the small car park in front of you towards a metal gate. Here is where the first, shorter variation re-joins the route. Go through the gap to the left of the gate to follow another white brick path up to a footpath sign. Notice the steep embankment on your right, indicating that there was once a railway line here.

Turn right at the footpath sign, and make your way down a short steep slope between the somewhat hidden remains of an old, red brick railway bridge. At the T-junction ahead, turn left. You are now on a wide woodland track with an embankment to your left and woodland to the right. Follow this track for 550 m until you come to Bepton Road.

14. Turn left onto Bepton Road, crossing over to walk on the pavement on the opposite side. After 350 m, you will see Station Road and arrive at the junction with New Road, both of which you should recognise from the start of the walk.

Cross the junction to retrace your steps back along the left hand side of Bepton Road. After 600 m, cross over at the pedestrian crossing. Bear left after the crossing and then turn right into West Street. Continue straight along West Street to arrive back at Market Square, where you started the walk.

THE SWAN INN

It is said that Midhurst once had the highest ratio of pubs to people of any town in England, and if you know where to look, you can see plenty of evidence to back up this claim.

Most of the premises that used to be pubs are now private residences, but The Swan is one of the handful that remain. Sitting on a road island between Red Lion Street and Church Hill, the pub and its accommodation span two Grade II listed buildings, which date back at least as far as the 17th Century, with some evidence to suggest that parts of each are a couple of hundred years older than this.

The pub is owned by the oldest independent brewer in Sussex, Harvey's Brewery. The current landlords, Digby and Katie Furneaux, have held the tenancy since January 2020. Weathering lockdown with inspiring positivity, this enterprising couple used the enforced closure to plough all of their energies into refurbishing the pub, inside and out. They rose phoenix-like in the Summer of 2020, with a completely new proposition for customers. Cigars and cocktails play a large part in the new offering, with accommodation designed to meet the needs of those looking for a weekend of shooting. The whole package is quirky; tradition offset against bold, modern design, with a side order of fun.

A FAMILY VENTURE

If you meet the Furneauxs, you will see this sense of fun reflected in them. They are a young family and have taken well to living right in the centre of Midhurst. You get the feeling that the town is just an extension of their backyard. The children play happily in Market Square and the dogs are walked on St. Ann's Hill. Sit on a bench in Market Square for any length of time on a Saturday morning and you will almost certainly see the Furneauxs going about their business.

It is their tenacity and enthusiasm for being part of the Midhurst community that has earned them a place in people's hearts. Not only have they revitalised The Swan, they also organised community events during lockdown, such as socially distanced carols on Christmas Eve. More recently, they organised a very successful Jazz Evening. Now they have a piano, no doubt there will be more great ideas to come from this energetic, young family, who have immersed themselves so fully and so quickly into Midhurst life.

GREAT FOOD AND A WARM WELCOME

The pub itself is well worth a visit. Comfortable seating inside and out, and a small, carefully chosen menu, makes it the perfect place to sit and relax with friends. Those who remember how The Swan used to be all agree that the changes are a huge improvement. Given that the pub is right next to the start and end point for the walks in this book, it would be rude not to pop in and see what they have to offer. Digby and Katie would be very pleased to see you.

THE ONE WITH LANDMARKS AND LEGACIES

On this route, there are local landmarks to look out for and interesting people to learn about as you walk between Midhurst and its neighbouring village, Stedham. There are formal and informal memorials to be found, buildings ready to reveal their history, and stories about the people who have, in one way or another, left a legacy for future generations.

Stedham is a pretty village just to the west of Midhurst. Like many small villages in the area, it has changed little over the centuries. Its name is of Saxon origin and is said to mean 'the water meadow where stallions graze'. This is depicted in the metalwork of the village sign, which can be seen at the intersection between The Street and School Lane.

The church also has Saxon origins, but most of what you see today dates back to either the 1850s or, in the case of the clock tower, the 1600s. Probably the oldest thing you can see anywhere in the village is the huge yew tree in the churchyard, which is thought to be over 2,500 years old.

In the early part of the 20th century, the Scrimgeour family moved to Stedham Hall. Over a number of years, they gifted the community a reading room, playing fields, and a bath house, and built several cottages for their workers. The Aubretia that is seen in many village gardens can also be attributed to the Scrimgeours, as it was said to be their favourite flower.

The route to Stedham takes you from Market Square in Midhurst, past the Caron Lane Cemetery, and over Sunset Hill. In all three locations you can see monuments to those in the armed forces, who lost their lives in combat over the years.

Following a trail across Midhurst Common, you cross the A272 to access Stedham via a polo field on its eastern edge. Walking around the village, you pass tiny cottages of various styles and ages. There are clues to the former use of some residencies, such as the Old Bakehouse and the Old Ale House. One cottage on the main street is called Aubretia Cottage, reflecting the link with the Scrimgeour family and their favourite flower.

On a sharp bend between the main street and the church, you will find a property called Tye Hill. Now completely renovated, until recently, it was empty, intimidating, and almost completely hidden by ivy. As a young teenager, I can remember being scared of going past it on walks down to Stedham Mill from my Auntie's shop on The Street.

Passing the church, with its ancient Yew, and the entrance to Stedham Hall, you arrive at Stedham Mill, a Grade II listed property in a beautifully scenic riverside setting. Crossing at the weir, you can choose a river path back to Midhurst or take a parallel trail high above it through National Trust woodland. Both are equally beautiful routes, so you may well find yourself doing this walk more than once.

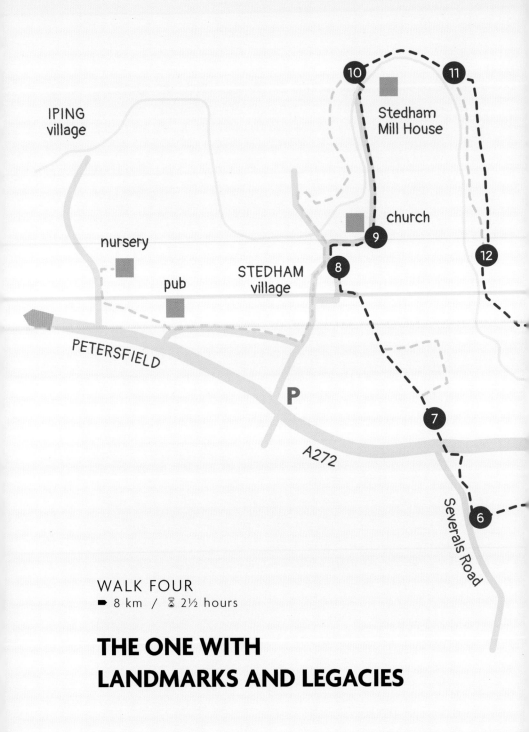

IPING
village

Stedham
Mill House

nursery

church

pub

STEDHAM
village

PETERSFIELD

P

A272

Severals Road

10

11

9

12

8

7

6

WALK FOUR
➡ 8 km / ⧗ 2½ hours

THE ONE WITH
LANDMARKS AND LEGACIES

1	route guide	⋰⋰	walk route
🌲🌳	woods	⋰⋰	alternative route
▪	site of interest	⋯	footpath/track
P	parking	▬	road

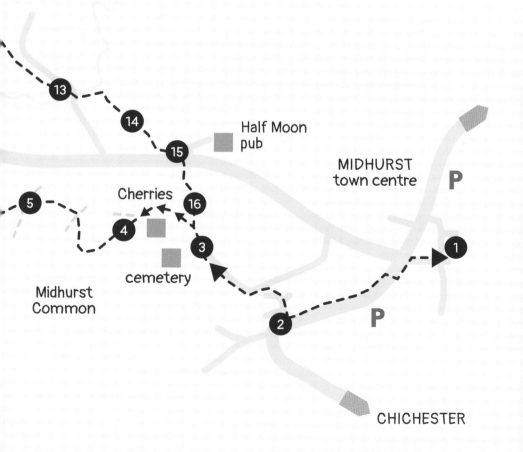

13

14

15

Half Moon
pub

**MIDHURST
town centre**

P

Cherries

5

16

1

4

3

cemetery

P

2

Midhurst
Common

CHICHESTER

➲ VARIATIONS

There are not many options to make this route shorter without driving the 4 km from Midhurst to Stedham. Parking in the village is limited, but you could leave your car in the layby on the A272, just a little way outside the village. You can then make your way down The Street to the village green and join the route at Point **8.** When you arrive at the mill, you could simply retrace your steps back to the village. Alternatively, follow the river (the opposite way from the main route), to arrive at Stedham Bridge. Walk up to Tye Hill, turn right, and make your way back down The Street to the layby.

There are a couple of options for extending the route. For example, you could explore the village in more depth, taking a walk down School Lane and sampling the Thai cuisine at The Hamilton Arms. Or, instead of walking past Tye Hill towards the church, you could head down the hill and take a footpath on the left, which will lead you to the tiny village of Iping. Once there, it is easiest to turn back and retrace your steps to re-join the main route back to Midhurst from Point **8.**

➲ AMENITIES

The Hamilton Arms and the Rotherhill Nursery Café are the only refreshment options in Stedham. Both are on the outskirts of the village and not included in the walk. To get to them, you need to head down School Lane. They are at the far end of the lane (a walk of about 700 m), and there is no easy option to link them back into the main route. So, once refreshed, you will need to retrace your steps.

➲ ROUTE GUIDE

1. Leave Market Square, making your way around to the left of The Swan Inn to head along West Street. Continue ahead for 100 m until you come to the junction with Bepton Road. Turn left and cross over at the pedestrian crossing. Turning again to your left, walk along the pavement, past the police station and a number of residencies.

Follow the road for 400 m, crossing the intersections with Ashfield Road and Heathfield Gardens. After the Heathfield Gardens intersection, Midhurst Primary School is on your right.

2. The next turning is Heathfield Park. Turn onto this road and head straight, with the school playing fields initially on your right. After 70 m, the road curves to the left. Ahead there is a footpath sign attached to a lamppost. The sign points to a tarmac path on the right that runs between two bungalows. This path is a shortcut that connects Heathfield Park with Carron Lane. Take this path, and after 20 m, follow it round to the left and out into a small parking area. Head across the parking area onto Carron Lane and turn left. Follow the road around to the right and steadily uphill to the Carron Lane Cemetery.

FOUR EXTRAORDINARY BROTHERS

When you reach the cemetery, you may like to take a short detour before continuing the walk. The cemetery is well maintained, with some old and beautiful headstones. One grave in particular reveals a sad story. It is the grave of John Cuthbert Garland, the last of four brothers, all of whom were killed whilst on active service during WWII. His gravestone is easy to find, and it lists the names of his brothers. To find it, walk along the wide gravel path from the cemetery entrance and take the first gravel path on the right. After 10 m, there are three military headstones on the left, and J.C. Garland's is the middle one. To continue the walk, retrace your steps and make a sharp turn to the left when you arrive back at the cemetery entrance.

3. Follow a wide track, with the boundary fence of the cemetery on your left. To your right, and ahead, there are woods. Keep straight as you pass two turnings to the left. The track curves to the left to arrive at the driveway to a property called Cherries. With this property on your left, continue along the track until you reach its wooden garage. Bear right, at a signposted fork 10 m beyond the garage, to head up a slight incline.

4. You are now on a relatively straight, level path that runs along the side of a wooded hill, with the ground sloping down to your left and up to your right. Continue on this path for 200 m until you see the trees start to thin ahead. The path curves to the right as you emerge from the trees, and there are two benches ahead.

AT THE GOING DOWN OF THE SUN....

This is Sunset Hill, and, weather permitting, there are views across the clearing towards the South Downs. Note the memorial tree, planted in memory of a local Marine, Corporal David O'Connor, who was killed in Afghanistan in 2012.

Keeping the benches on your right, continue around the edge of the hill for another 150 m. You will see a third bench ahead. Make your way around it, as if to sit on it, and note two paths in front of you. Take the right-hand path, which descends steeply to bring you to a footpath crossroad. Head straight across on a path that continues to descend, although less steeply than before.

5. After 120 m, turn left onto a track that leads to the property on your right. Bear left 50 m ahead, as the track curves to the right. You are now on a wide woodland trail with pine trees all around. After 100 m, you come to a point where several paths meet. Take the second path from the left, and continue through the woods for another 200 m, to arrive at a metal gate beside Severals Road.

6. Turn right onto Severals Road and follow it for 300 m. As the road curves to the left, there is a narrow footpath on the right. Head down this path for 100 m until you come to the A272. Turn left and walk along the tarmac path.

Ahead, on the opposite side of the road, there is a footpath. It is well hidden by the hedgerows which can sometimes become overgrown, so look carefully for the sign. As there is no walkway on the other side of the road, you should not cross until you have seen the footpath, and are right opposite it.

If you get as far as the layby (also on the opposite side of the road), you have gone too far. When you are level with the footpath sign, cross the road and head down through the gap in the trees.

7.　　The path descends gently through woodland. Keep straight after 100 m, at what looks like a crossroad. Continue to a wooden bridge 50 m further on, then exit the woods beside an access road.

The road skirts a polo field. The field itself is higher than the road, so head up the flight of wooden steps in front of you. Make your way across the field towards a row of white cottages. If the field is in use, walk back down the steps and follow the alternate footpath around the field, as shown on the map.

On the far side of the polo field, cross the access road again and continue your route across a second field. When you reach the edge of this field, go through the gap in the hedge and follow a gravel path in front of the white cottages of Lavender Row.

This path quickly becomes an access road, which in turn meets a narrow lane called The Alley. The Old Bakehouse is on your right and a property called Alley Studios is ahead of you. Turn right to walk down this pretty lane, noting the old stone cottages and the terrace of houses built in 1886.

8.　　After 100 m, the lane curves to the left to intersect with The Street (the main road through the village). To explore the village further, follow the variation described below. To continue the main route, bear right onto The Street and then keep right at a fork to follow Mill Road, past a brick and timber property called Tye Hill.

See More of the Village　▶　Turn left onto The Street and follow it for 500 m until you reach School Lane. As you make your way through the village towards School Lane you will pass by the former location of the village shop, which is next door to The Old Ale House (both now private residencies). You will also pass the village green, the old bath house, and Aubretia Cottage.

WALK FOUR - DETAILED MAP
Stedham village

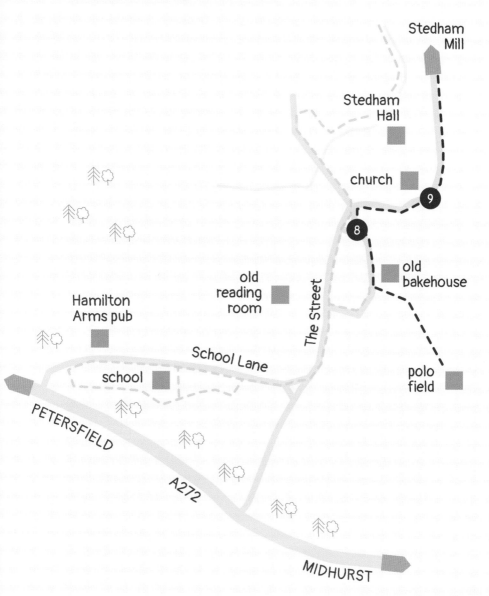

When you arrive at the turning for School Lane, you will see the Stedham Village sign, depicting its stallion in the water meadow. You can turn around here and retrace your steps or continue down School Lane. Bear in mind that you will eventually need to retrace your steps to get back to the main route.

The only option that avoids this, without making the walk very lengthy, is joining Iping Lane beyond Rotherhill Nursery, and walking along the road into Iping (600 m). From here, you can find a footpath that will bring you back to Stedham. When you arrive at Stedham Bridge, turn right and walk up the road towards Tye Hill.

Follow the road around to the right, all the way past Tye Hill. As you round the bend you see the graveyard of St. James' Church ahead on the left. The church sits a metre or so above the road, its graveyard actually spanning the land on both sides. It is worth pausing for a few minutes to explore.

A SUBMARINER WITH A STORY

The first thing you will see is the ancient yew tree. Large and impressive, it also has a hollow trunk. It is said that one former groundsman kept his tools inside it. If you explore the graveyard further, you will find the grave of Commander Norman Holbrook. It can be found on the other side of the church from the yew tree. A former owner of Stedham Mill, Commander Holbrook was the first submariner to be awarded the Victoria Cross. His story is one that is worth reading up on to learn more.

9. Follow Mill Road past the church and around a sharp left-hand bend. Fields lie beyond the hedgerows on the right, and after 100 m, you get a fleeting view of Stedham Hall on your left. You can get a better view of it from the opposite side if you take the footpath from Stedham Mill along the river to Stedham Bridge. This is an optional extension on this walk and also the route used in Walk Five.

THE PUBLIC FOOTPATH PRIVILEGE

Continue along the road as it passes cottages on the right and stables on the left. These buildings give way to fields, and up ahead, the driveway to Stedham Mill awaits. It is a privilege to be able to walk down the driveway to Stedham Mill and share its beautiful setting in a way that is not always possible with a private residence.

Public footpaths often cross private land, and the right to walk these routes is a gift passed down through the generations, and one that should not be taken for granted. At the foot of the driveway, bear left in front of the house to make your way over the weir and onto a path beside a small grassed area.

This is the best point from which to admire the perfectly landscaped gardens rising behind the mill house and along the river on either side of the weir.

10. Having crossed the river at the weir, head towards the steep wooded hill in front of you. A fence on the right marks the boundary of the mill house garden. One footpath heads up the steep hill and the other turns right on level ground alongside the boundary fence. Follow the level path, with the river on your right and woodland to your left. After 200 m, cross a wooden bridge and continue for another 150 m until you see a flight of steps on your left.

Here is where you have a choice. You can continue along beside the river or head up the steps to take a woodland route. The river route is simpler to follow, so the notes below describe the woodland option. The sketch map shows both paths.

11. Climb through the trees, at first on the steep steps and then on a path, until you meet a wide woodland track at the top of the slope. Turn right and head straight through the woods for 700 m. The main route is clear and you should find it easy to ignore the trails that lead off to the left and right.

The correct path keeps to the steep wooded slope that falls away to your right. The river is at the bottom of this slope, and you may catch glimpses of it as you make your way along. In spring, bluebells make a lovely display on both sides of this woodland path.

12. After 500 m, the path descends gradually and 200 m further along you will see a short wooden fence ahead. Turn right to head down to a gate and re-join the river footpath. Go through the gate and turn left. After 120 m go through another gate into a large field.

The path through the field initially runs parallel to the fence on your left. As the field opens out to the left, keep slightly right to pass by a five-bar gate, and skirt the hedge ahead of you. As you come around the hedge, continue to make your way around the field towards a gate and a stone bridge on the far side.

13. The bridge is medieval and in remarkably good condition for its age. Take care to listen out for cars as you pass through the gate and onto the road to cross the bridge. On the far side of the bridge, there is a footpath on the left. Go through the gate and follow the path, with the river on your left. After 85 m, the path turns sharply to the right and comes to a gate. Pass through the gate to continue up a slope and out into an open field.

14. Keeping the fence to your left, head straight across a footpath crossroads and continue to follow the fence line to a gate in the corner of the field. Go through this gate and into a much smaller field. On the far side of this field, just beyond a metal gate, there is a wooden bridge on the right. Cross over, and follow the marked footpath out onto a path beside the A272.

15. Turn left onto the path and head towards the Half Moon Pub. As you arrive at the junction with June Lane, turn to your right to cross the A272. On the opposite side of the road there are two footpaths heading into the woods. These two paths run almost parallel to each other, and it does not matter which one you take. Head up through the trees until you come out into a clearing with a bench on the opposite side. Cross the clearing, keeping the bench on your left.

16. Keep straight ahead at the footpath crossroads and then bear left as this path merges with a track from the right. As you turn onto this track, the Carron Lane Cemetery is on your right. Continue ahead to retrace your steps down Carron Lane and around the left-hand bend until you see the green footpath sign directing you back between the bungalows to Heathfield Park.

Turn left as you emerge from the cut through and follow Heathfield Park around to the right to the junction with Bepton Road. Turn left onto Bepton Road and follow it for 500 m until you come to the pedestrian crossing. Cross over and turn to your left, then turn right at the mini roundabout to walk down West Street and back to Market Square.

WALKING WITH CHILDREN

Walking is a beneficial activity for almost anyone at almost any age. We benefit physically and emotionally when we are outdoors, surrounded by nature. This is especially true for children.

Encouraging children to walk on a regular basis builds good habits for a fit and healthy lifestyle. It also provides opportunities to understand the environmental challenges we face today.

As we all continue to recognise the importance of green spaces and the wildlife that inhabit them, it is our children who will eventually take responsibility for ensuring that they are protected and nurtured. With many species in the UK already facing severe decline, and even extinction, it is hugely important that young people engage with the issues and care enough to try to fix them.

So, how best to cultivate a love of the outdoors when faced with a child who declares that they do not like walking? One way to do this is to make walking a regular part of family life; something pleasant that brings the whole family together to have fun.

MAKING IT FUN

Take short walks with plenty of interesting things to see and do along the way; things that the whole family will happily take part in. It could be as simple as counting how many birds, butterflies, and flowers you see. You could collect leaves, feathers, and eggshells to identify later or take photographs to document your rambles.

For children who are particularly hard to tear away from their electronic devices, you could try geocaching. This is a fun way to introduce children to maps, co-ordinates, and puzzles as they attempt to discover hidden 'booty' in the outdoors.

On the best of our summer days, picnics are a great way to entice children outdoors. There is something rather lovely about eating outdoors in the sunshine, particularly if the whole family have been involved in packing the picnic.

Those who are more adventurous might consider an evening walk, 'picnicking' perhaps on hot chocolate that you make on a camping stove. There are a number of lightweight stoves on the market that would enable you to enjoy this activity without endangering yourself or the environment around you.

GET WITH THE PROGRAMME

If you feel daunted 'going it alone', there are plenty of organisations that run child-centred outdoor activities, especially during school holidays. Many organisations recognise the key role that technology plays in our lives today and very successfully bring the natural and the digital together in ways that help children to engage more easily.

With all the above in mind, all the walks in this book have activity sheets to accompany them. These can be downloaded from the Finding Footpaths website (**findingfootpaths.com**). Designed with children in mind, there are specific items to look out for and various challenges to complete. There is also a Finding Footpaths group on Facebook, where you can post about your walks, sharing photos, questions, and comments.

Finding pleasure in walking together as a family is one of the simplest things you can do to keep your children active and engaged with nature. As a generation, they will face some tough environmental challenges. Their willingness to find solutions will be influenced by their experiences. Teaching them to value green spaces and wildlife might just help them reverse some of the damage that has already been done.

MAKING PROGRESS

Be encouraged and excited by attempting longer walks. It is a privilege to start your journey in town, walk for 18 or more kilometres, and never cross a road bigger than a country lane.

It is a pleasure to start your day early, especially in summer when the footpaths are dry and the sun is gently warming your back. You arrive at the halfway point of your walk, somewhere remote and peaceful, to sip from a flask of coffee and admire the views before most folks are even out of bed.

The walks in the second part of this book are longer than those in the first section, and the route descriptions are a little less detailed. However, you will still find variations that allow you to shorten or lengthen each main route.

The aim is to take you deeper into the countryside and some distance away from Midhurst. if you're not ready to go that far, the shorter variations will give you a great introduction, without taking up too much of your time or energy.

There is a good chance you won't see anyone else as you traverse these quiet footpaths, which means you are likely to see plenty of wildlife. Take a picnic or a flask.

Pause. Listen. Watch. Breathe deeply.

These are the walks with the power to revitalise you.

WALK FIVE / ➡ 18 km / ⏳ 5½ hours

THE ONE WITH THE BIG HILL

This is a classic English countryside walk, at its best
on a hot summer's day when you can take your time
to wander lazily through the beautiful landscape.
Lie under a tree or linger at the top of Older Hill
for a picnic lunch. Listen to the river as it gurgles
and bubbles along beside you. Watch butterflies as
they flit tantalisingly ahead of you, leading the way
through woods and long grass.

This walk begins alongside the River Rother from Woolbeding,
into Stedham and then on to Iping. It continues through woodland
that becomes increasingly reminiscent of Tolkien's Rivendell before
arriving just shy of the halfway point outside the hamlet of Redford.

From here, there is a short but steep climb up to the top of
Older Hill and sweeping views of the South Downs. Spend a little
time absorbing these views as you make your way around the rim of
this broad valley and onto Woolbeding Common.

The woodland eventually gives way to heathland that is at its
best in late summer when the bracken and heather sit side by side
in resplendent colour.

The route back down to the river is a much gentler gradient than
the climb up, and farmland replaces heath before setting you back on
course to retrace your steps along the river to the start point.

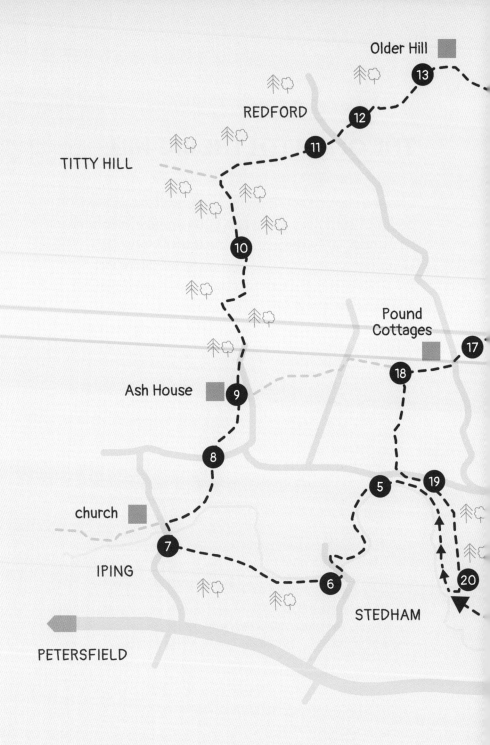

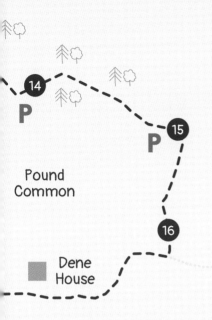

THE ONE WITH
THE BIG HILL

14

P

15

P

Pound
Common

16

■ Dene
House

1	route guide	⟋	walk route
🌲🌳	woods	⟋	alternative route
■	site of interest	⋰	footpath/track
P	parking	▬	road

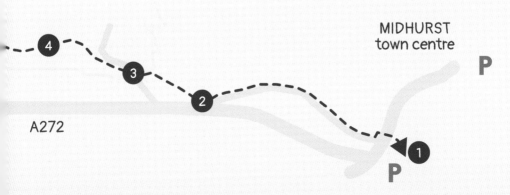

MIDHURST
town centre

P

4

3

2

1

P

A272

➲ VARIATIONS

Two shorter variations are suggested, and both enable you to miss out the 'big hill' that defines this walk. The climb to the top of Older Hill is steep, so perhaps not for everyone. If you are keen to see the views but unable to complete the whole walk or the steep climb, you can explore the hill more easily from one of the two nearby parking areas marked on the route map.

The shortest variation goes only as far as Stedham Mill (Point **5.**), where you can turn away from the river up a steep path and re-join the walk at Point **19.** This variation can be completed in around 2 hours.

The second option is to leave the walk at Ash House (Point **9.**) and follow footpaths in an easterly direction across fields until you can re-join the walk at Point **18.** This route will take 3½ hours.

JOIN TWO WALKS TOGETHER

If you want to make the route longer, you can take a turning on the left part way through Point **14.** This enables you to switch to Walk Six as it passes Scotland Farmhouse, walking it in reverse back to Easebourne and on into Midhurst.

VISIT CHITHURST MONESTARY

Another option is to continue west, from Iping church into Chithurst. Making your way around the manor house and Buddhist monastery, you can follow a path through Hammer Wood and onto Moorhouse Lane.

This will connect with the Serpent Trail just north of Robins Farm and bring you to Titty Hill, where you can re-join the main route at Point **10.** This extension will add another 5 km / 1½ hours to your walk.

➲ AMENITIES

There are no shops, cafés, or pubs along this route, so take plenty of food and water with you.

➲ ROUTE GUIDE

1. From Market Square, follow Church Hill past the church and around to the left into Knockhundred Row. At the junction with North Street, turn right. Cross at the pedestrian crossing, turning to the left on the opposite side. Make your way back up North Street until you reach the intersection with June Lane. Follow this road for 1 km until it comes to a T-junction with the A272 Petersfield Road.

2. Turn right along a tarmac pavement. As this pavement ends, take a marked footpath on the right. Follow this path across rough ground, over a wooden bridge, and into a small field. On the far side of the field, go through a gate into a larger, second field.

After 100 m, head straight across a footpath crossroad to descend between a row of trees and a fence. Ahead there is a gate, and as you pass through it, the path turns sharply to the left. The River Rother is now on your right. Follow this path for 90 m until you come to a gate beside a stone bridge.

3. This is Woolbeding Bridge. It is medieval and single-track. Wait until there is no traffic before crossing. On the far side, turn left to go through a gate and into a field. Follow a trail through the grass, keeping near to the fence line at first. After 250 m, the field will open out a little on your right, as you pass a five bar gate. Continue straight for a further 250 m to the far side of the field, where there is another gate.

4. Pass through the gate to follow a track on the edge of woodland and alongside the river, which is now close by on your left. The path follows the river closely for 1 km before arriving at Stedham Mill. Along the route, there is another gate and a wooden bridge to mark your progress.

It is quite common to see deer in the woods to your right or on the open land on the opposite side of the river. Kingfishers have been known to nest here, and during spring and summer, it is a haven for butterflies.

5.   Stedham Mill marks the point of the first (and shortest) variation to the route. To follow it, look for a steep path on the right as you draw level with the weir and follow the directions below.

Get Home Quicker ▶   Take the steep path on your right and follow it up through dense woodland for 150 m until it meets a country lane. Turn right onto the lane and follow it as it bends to the right. Just after the bend, take an unmarked footpath on the right to enter a wood. Now skip ahead to Point **19.** to follow the main route back into Midhurst.

To continue the main route, turn left and make your way around the edge of a clearing, which, in spring, is full of wildflowers. Keep the river on your left as you pass through a gap in the hedgerow on the far side of the clearing and out into a large field. Follow the path along the edge of this field, with the river on your left.

After 500 m, the large, timber-framed rear elevation of Stedham Hall is visible on the opposite bank. After passing the hall and its grounds, continue on the path as it turns sharp right, away from the river, and then sharp left into a small (unofficial) parking area. Head straight towards the road and turn left onto it. Pass Bridgefoot Farm on your right and a row of cottages on your left, then cross over Stedham Bridge.

6.   On the far side of the bridge, turn right onto a footpath. As you begin to follow this path, the river will be on your right. After 450 m, the river makes a deep bend to the right, away from the path, and the landscape changes from woodland to fields. Continue on the path for a further 550 m to arrive at a metal gate and a row of cottages.

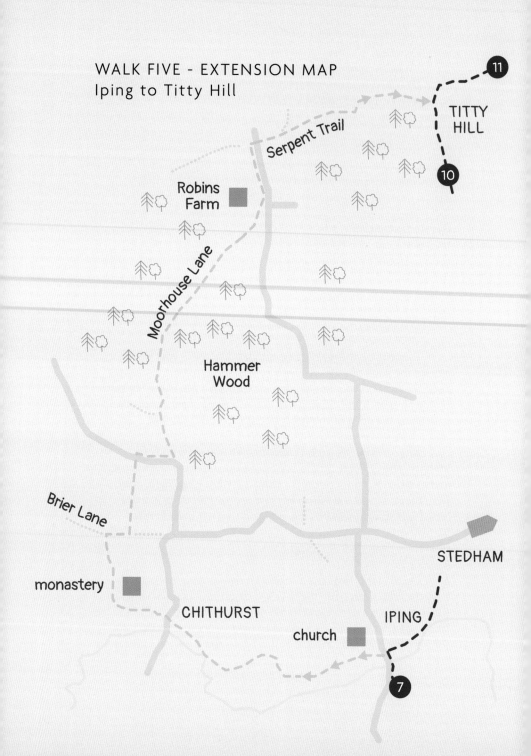

WALK FIVE - EXTENSION MAP
Iping to Titty Hill

Go through the gate and follow the gravel track to walk past the end of Coachman's Cottage. Cross in front of the gates leading to Stable Cottage and Iping House and make your way down a steep cobbled pathway to a road.

7. Turn right onto the road and follow it around to the left and over a stone bridge. This is Iping. Continue along the road towards the church. If you are planning to extend the route out to Chithurst, follow the directions below and re-join the main route at Point **10.**

Stay Out Longer ▶ Walk through the churchyard, keeping the church on your right. On the far side of the churchyard is a gate leading into a field. Follow the footpath for 1 km across fields until you meet a country lane. Opposite and slightly right is another footpath. This path quickly turns to the right and then to the left before crossing an open field. On the opposite side of the field, cross a stile into another field and immediately turn right to follow the fence line.

Follow the path for 300 m until it meets a wide track (Brier Lane). Turn right onto the track, and then after 100 m, turn left onto another footpath. After 400 m, turn right onto a country lane. As this lane bends sharply to the right, turn left onto another wide track (Moorhouse Lane). Follow this track for 1.6 km until it meets a tarmac road at Robins Farm. Turn left onto the road and follow it for 350 m until you see a footpath on the right with a waymarker for the Serpent Trail. Continue on this trail for 1 km to arrive at the cottages of Titty Hill, where you can re-join the main route at Point **10.**

To continue the main route, take the marked footpath opposite the church. Pass through the wooden gate and make your way around the edge of two adjacent fields, both kitted out with jumps and other obstacles associated with equestrian eventing. There are two styles to navigate, one between the two fields and another at the far corner of the second field. After crossing the second style, head down a short slope towards a single-track road.

8.   Opposite and slightly to the right, there is a signposted footpath. It rises steeply through a wood that is also used for eventing. Make sure you are on the correct path here; there are several tracks leading away from the road but only one that is a public footpath. The correct path is straight ahead as you cross the road. It heads up steeply and then along the side of a hill that overlooks a grass valley on the left. After 500 m, this path ends beside the driveway to Ash House.

9.   As you step down from the footpath, you are at the junction between the driveway for Ash House and its access road. Here is your second opportunity to shorten the walk by following the description below and re-joining the main route at Point **18.**

Get Home Quicker ▶ Cross the driveway entrance. On the opposite side of the access road is a footpath. Follow this path up a steep slope and into woodland. After 75 m, the path curves to the left and then comes to a junction. Bear right to continue up the slope and onto a track between two fields.

After 350 m, the track comes to a road beside a cottage with various outbuildings. Turn left onto the road and follow it for 100 m, past a modern single-storey home built around a courtyard. Turn right onto a footpath that runs along the boundary of this property.

There is a large field on your left and hedgerows to the right. Halfway across the field (300 m), there is a footpath on your right. This is where you re-join the main route. Follow the notes in Point **18.** from the instruction to "Follow this path for 800 m as it descends gradually through the fields to meet a road".

If you are continuing the main route, turn left to follow the road until you come to Ash Cottage. With the cottage directly in front of you, turn left and then right to follow a restricted byway along the side of the property and on into the woods. Keep following the maroon-coloured markers for this restricted byway through the woods, ignoring all paths to the left and right.

10. After 450 m, the path bends deeply to the right and continues along the bottom of a deep cutting. At this point, the path is often very muddy, and you will need to navigate around the boggiest parts.

RIVENDELL'S BEAUTY IN WEST SUSSEX

Continue for a further 450 m until you see a house on the right. The path now becomes a track and there is a drystone wall on the right. This wall separates you from a beautiful pine tree wood.

After 350 m, keep straight to continue on the restricted byway, ignoring the footpath on the right. Keep straight again as a footpath joins from the left. Keep ahead for another 100 m until you see the cottages of the tiny hamlet called Titty Hill. There are three properties alongside the track as it takes a deep bend to the right.

This is the point where the longer variation (via Chithurst) re-joins the route. Just after the bend, take a footpath on the right to head into a copse. This footpath is signposted for the Serpent Trail. Follow this trail for 800 m until you come to the road just outside Redford.

© SDNPA

11. Cross over to follow a private road up a short steep incline and then bear left at the fork towards a property called Hookland. Opposite the driveway for Hookland Farmhouse, turn right onto a footpath that leads steeply up between bracken and brambles. After a short, steep climb, you emerge onto a track in front of Barnetts Cottage.

12. With Barnetts Cottage in front of you, take the second footpath from the left. This path rises steeply between three large oak trees. Bear left at a fork beside the third oak tree to follow the path upwards along a ridge with wooded slopes falling away to the left and right. After a steep 200 m climb, you arrive at the top of the hill beside a wooden bench.

13. With the bench behind you, follow the grass path ahead. It quickly splits around a cluster of shrubs and small trees. It does not matter which branch you take because both paths meet again after 30 m or so. However, the right-hand path has better views and is the recommended route.

FEAST ON THE VIEWS

The Serpent Trail joins from the right as the path curves to the right, taking you around the rim of the valley. On a clear day, there are sweeping views from here all the way to the South Downs. It is the perfect place for a picnic or a leisurely break.

After 200 m, turn left and then immediately right onto a metalled road. Follow the road for 200 m until you arrive at a parking area on the left. Opposite the car park and across a small, grassed area, there is a wooden bench and a viewpoint.

14. Admire the views and then retrace your steps to cross the car park. Take the footpath immediately to the left of the information board. This path is marked for the Serpent Trail and the Lipchis Way. After 100 m, the path meets a sandy track.

Bear left on this track as it heads up a steady incline to meet a dirt road. Just before the track meets the road, look out for two sandstone sculptures, one on either side of the track. Named 'Resting Reptiles', they are part of a sculpture trail across seven lowland heath sites in the National Park. Turn right on to the dirt road. If you would like to connect this walk with Walk Six, follow the variation below.

Stay Out Longer ▶ Continue on the dirt road for 250 m, then turn left onto a track that almost immediately bends sharply to the right. Ahead are the buildings of Scotland Farmhouse. Before you get to the buildings, cross the stile on your left to head across a field. You are now on the route for Walk Six at Point **16.** and can walk it in reverse all the way back to Midhurst.

To continue the main route, follow the road for 500 m until you come to an unmarked, off-road parking area on your right. Ignore the first entrance but take the second and almost immediately take a footpath on the left that is marked for the Lipchis Way.

15.   Follow the path through woodland, with a dry-stone wall to your left. After 400 m, keep left at a fork on a faint path through the woods. Keep left again after 70 m to take a sandy path out onto heathland that has heather and bracken to the left and right.

Along the route from the car park to the heath, you might become aware of a wider track on your right. Use this track as a reference to make sure you're on the much prettier, but narrower and quieter, footpath.

16.   Continue across the open heath for 350 m, keeping straight at a footpath crossroad and turning right at a T-junction 30 m further ahead. With a dry-stone wall separating you from the farmland on your left, follow this path for 700 m until the wall is replaced by the wooden fence around a property called Dene House. Once again, you may notice a wide track to the right of the path you are on. Stick to the path, staying close to the drystone wall for a quieter, prettier route.

17.   Follow the fence around Dene House and then turn left onto a track that rises steeply. Continue along the track for 200 m until you reach a small parking area and a road. On the opposite side of the road is a property called Pound Common Cottages, and to the right of this there is a marked footpath. Take this path through a small copse and out into farmland beyond. Follow the track between two fields, with the hedgerows to your left.

18.   After 150 m, turn left onto another footpath, also between two fields. This time the hedgerows are on your right. This is the point where the second shorter variation re-joins the route. Follow this path for 800 m as it descends gradually through the fields to meet a road. Turn left onto the road. Follow it around a right-hand bend and then take an unmarked footpath on the right to enter a wood.

19. Follow the footpath through the woods for 250 m, ignoring any small trails off to the left or right. Bear right as you come to Brambling Farm, keeping a large barn on your left as you continue through the wood.

The path heads straight along the top of a slope that falls away steeply to your right. At the bottom of this slope is the river that you walked beside at the start of the walk. After 750 m, turn right just before the path arrives at a short stretch of wooden fencing. Head down a steep slope to a gate.

20. Go through the gate and turn left onto another footpath. This is the path you were on at the start of the walk. Retrace your steps through the gate and across the fields to Woolbeding Bridge. Cross the bridge and, continuing to retrace your steps, turn left onto the footpath beside the river.

Follow the path as it turns sharply to the right and up a steady slope with trees on either side. After 75 m, you emerge from the ·trees into a field. Keep straight at the footpath crossroad ahead to arrive at the far side of the field. Head through the gate into a second, smaller field, and back out to the A272. Turn left to walk beside the road, towards the junction with June Lane.

21. Turn left down June Lane and follow it back into town to emerge once again on North Street. Turn left and walk past the shops to cross at the pedestrian crossing. Turn right to head back up North Street and then turn left onto Knockhundred Row. Follow the road around to the right as it becomes Church Hill. Continue past the church to arrive back at Market Square.

TILLY'S OF MIDHURST

Tilly's is the place to go for exquisite afternoon teas. They serve excellent lunches too, but it's the array of beautifully crafted cakes that really makes Tilly's stand out when it comes to tea-time indulgences.

Husband and wife team, Neil and Teresa, took on the premises in Rumbolds Hill in 2018. Its conversion from bank to tea room had not long been completed, but Neil and Teresa were keen to put their own stamp on it. A subtle uplift to the décor successfully introduced a modern twist without losing the homey feel. The menu underwent a more radical overhaul, a clear sign that something new and exciting was on the way.

A trained chef with more than 30 years' experience, Neil delights in having an outlet for his creative talents. His mouth-watering dishes take advantage of locally sourced, seasonal produce wherever possible, and whether you are looking for salad, soup, or something more substantial, you are guaranteed generous portions and flawless presentation.

It is the care with which everything at Tilly's is presented that speaks volumes about the passion behind this business. Neil himself confesses that his heart lies with the delicious works of art that are his cakes, but his five-star background shines through everything that comes out of his kitchen.

Whilst Neil is busy cooking, it is Teresa who looks after everything front of house. With her background in hospitality, she strikes a perfect balance between a friendly welcome and professional courtesy. Single-handedly managing seated customers, as well as takeaway orders, Teresa undoubtedly plays an equal part in ensuring the smooth-running success of the business.

FIT FOR A QUEEN

This talented duo has brought something very special to Midhurst. Much more than a tearoom, sitting somewhere between a café and a restaurant, Tilly's is the place to experience quality in a relaxed, informal setting. Given that Neil has in the past cooked for the Queen Mother, he can truly claim that his food is fit for a queen, and when you have tasted his cakes, you are sure to agree.

THE ONE WITH THE ANCIENT WOODLAND

This walk takes you through and then high above the village of Easebourne to see some outstanding views of the South Downs. As you walk up towards Loves Farm, across to Vining, and then up Hoe Hill, you will see the Downs stretching away towards Amberley in the East and Petersfield in the West.

Seeing such a large section of the South Downs in a single vista, you can fully appreciate the unique characteristics that made them worthy of their National Park status. You might also ponder how comparatively little they have changed since they were first populated back in ancient times. A significant landmark well before the Romans built their villas, they are still every bit as striking today.

After climbing Hoe Hill, the route drops down into the steep and wooded terrain of Ovis and Bexleyhill Commons and then into Verdley Wood. This landscape is a superb contrast to the open views at the start of the walk. It is no less spectacular for enveloping you in dense woodland, as the tall pines and coppices make for a beautifully tranquil experience.

Passing The Duke of Cumberland Arms at roughly the halfway point of the walk is a happy accident that might just entice thirsty walkers to take a break. Rest a while in the delightful gardens before continuing through Northpark Copse, where there are views towards Black Down, the highest point in the South Downs National Park.

The South Downs once again come into view as you make your way across the heathland of Woolbeding Common and into Lord's Common. Here, you pass along the southern edge of the old and distinctive King Edward VII hospital. Designed by H. Percy Adams in 1902, it opened in 1906 and closed 100 years later. A remarkable hospital, it has now been converted into luxury residencies.

Re-entering Easebourne, via Whitters Farm and Budgeoner Hill, you will retrace your steps back past the church, farm shop, and polo fields before arriving back in Midhurst via Cowdray ruins.

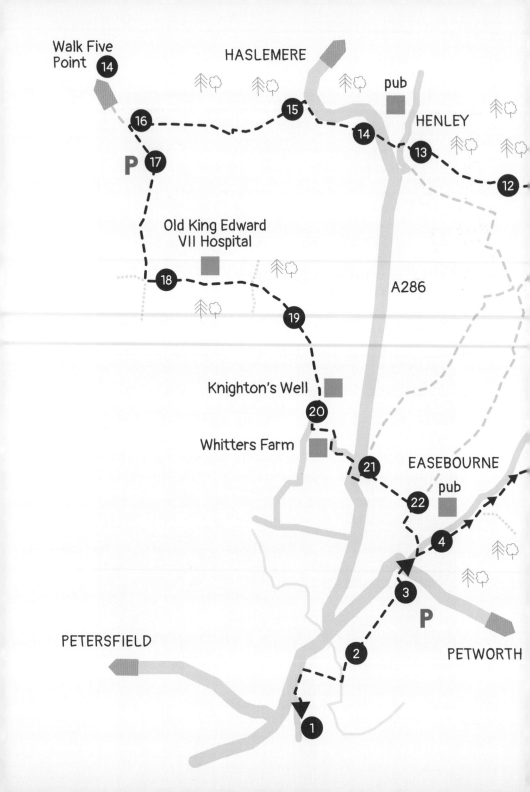

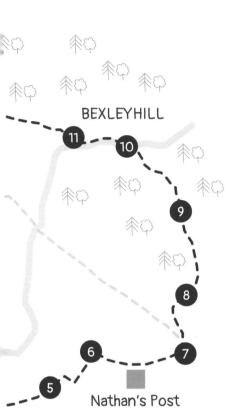

BEXLEYHILL

Nathan's Post

THE ONE WITH THE ANCIENT WOODLAND

1 route guide		✏ walk route	
🌲 woods		alternative route	
◼ site of interest		footpath/track	
P parking		🛣 road	

⮑ VARIATIONS

Two shorter variations are described for this route. The first diverts from the main route just after Upper Vining to pass through Vining Common and Vining Rough. Crossing Easebourne Street well outside the village itself, you then pass through Whitters Copse and walk across gently sloping fields back to Easebourne. This variation will take just over 2 hours to complete.

A second opportunity to shorten the walk comes as you reach Henley. Instead of crossing the A286, you head up steep steps and along the ridge of Verdley Hill towards Verdley Farm. Passing through the entertainingly named Scotland Knob, the track continues along the edge of woodland until you re-join the main route after it crosses the A286 by Budgenor Lodge. This variation takes around 3½ hours to complete.

Both shorter variations can be shortened a little further by starting and ending in Easebourne rather than Midhurst. If you wish to do this, it is possible to park in the large car park opposite the Cowdray Farm Shop & Café.

You can extend the walk by combining it with Walk Five. To do this, turn right instead of left as you reach the track after Scotland Farmhouse and follow the description for Walk Five in reverse from Point **14.** This creates a return route to Midhurst via Older Hill, Iping, and Stedham.

⮑ AMENITIES

There are various eateries and shops at the start and end of the walk in Midhurst and Easebourne. There is also a water tap on Easebourne Street just opposite the village store. As mentioned above, there is an excellent mid-route rest point at The Duke of Cumberland Arms. However, there are no other amenities on the route, so plan accordingly. It is a long route, so you are advised to take plenty of water.

⮌ ROUTE GUIDE

1.   Make your way from Market Square to Cowdray Ruins either by following the description in Walk Two or by walking through the town, as described below.

Turn right in front of the church and follow the road around to the left, past the Midhurst Museum to the junction with North Street. Turn right and walk down North Street to the second of two pedestrian crossings. Turn right between a cottage and a computer shop to access North Street Car Park via its pedestrian entrance. Head slightly left across the vehicle entrance to pass through a gate and onto the causeway that leads to Cowdray Ruins.

Cross two stone bridges and then turn left on an access road in front of the ruins. Head along this road, keeping the ruins and their boundary fence on your right. As the road bends to the left, continue straight ahead on a dirt track, with the cricket nets on your right and a double five-bar gate ahead.

2.   Go through the gap to the left of the gate and follow a wide track up a slope. There are polo fields to your right, visible all the way along this track as it first rises and then heads down towards Cowdray Farm Shop & Café.

Walk past the entrance to the shop and café and then take the gravel path on your left to walk towards and then in front of what was Easebourne Priory. This large stone property is easily recognised, with its three gable rooftops and mullion windows. A section of it is now the vicarage for the Parish Church of St. Mary.

3.   Pass in front of the vicarage and through the gap in the stone wall ahead to access the churchyard. Follow the gravel path round to the left and then to the right to exit the churchyard by the lichgate. Cross the road, bearing left as you do so to take the turning into Easebourne Street.

Pass the village store and The White Horse pub. Note the turning on the left after the pub for Glaziers Lane. This is where the route comes out into Easebourne Street at the end of the walk.

4.   Continue along Easebourne Street. It has no pavement but is a safe and enjoyable walk past numerous old and beautiful properties of all sizes. The properties belonging to the Cowdray estate are easily identified by their golden-yellow doors and window frames.

After 750 m, pass by the road on the left beside a Cowdray property called Holly Cottage. Remain on Easebourne Street as it bends deeply to the right and begins to rise more steeply. After a further 250 m, turn right onto an access road signposted for Loves Farm B&B and the House of Shaws. This road rises steeply, and as you climb higher, views of the South Downs stretch away to your right and behind you.

5.   Continue past driveways on the right, for Loves Farm and Lower Vining Barn, as the road becomes a track. Follow this track around to the right to skirt the boundary of two Cowdray cottages. As you walk around the side of the cottages, the track becomes a footpath. Head towards a post and wire fence and then turn sharply left alongside it. Continue along the edge of a field, with the wire fence on your right and hedgerows on your left.

6.   At the far side of the field, go through a gate and turn right onto a wide track. There are fields on both sides of this track and extensive views of the South Downs to the right. Keep straight, noting a memorial sculpture of a violin and fox along the way.

The sculpture is called Nathan's Post. It is in memory of Lord Nathan, who was chairman of the Sussex Downs Conservation Board. This was the forerunner of the South Downs National Park Authority. The inscription is taken from a poem by Hilaire Belloc:

"He does not die who can bequeath some influence to the land he knows." by Hilaire Belloc

7. Continue on the track until you reach the boundary fence of a property called Upper Vining. Keep straight to take a grass path beside the fence as the track bends away to the right. As you draw level with the house, the path drops steeply down to a track. Turn left onto this track and follow it around to the right and then towards a bench and footpath sign ahead.

Two paths cross here, and if you are going to complete the full walk, you need to go straight across the crossroad and down into the woodland ahead. If you want to take the first, shorter variation, turn left at the crossroad and follow the description below.

Get Home Quicker ▶ Follow the track along the edge of woodland for 450 m. As you draw level with the farm buildings on your left, bear left at the fork to cross a large field. On the far side of the field, enter the woods and keep straight for 600 m until you come to a country lane (Easebourne Street). Cross the lane to take the road opposite and follow it as it curves to the left. After 350 m, turn left onto a wide woodland path. Keep straight on this path for 700 m until you reach a T-junction at the far side of the woods.

Turn left along the edge of the wood, and after 100 m, bear right to exit the woods and head across farm fields towards Easebourne. Continue straight for 1.6 km as this path continues its gradual descent. At roughly the half way point, you arrive at a crossroad. Go straight across to continue on a path that is in a deep cutting. After 400 m, you emerge from the cutting again and are able to see the fields on either side. Keep straight for another 400 m until you see a path coming from the right. This is the T-junction mentioned at the end of Point **21.** Skip ahead to Point **22.** to finish the walk on the main route.

8. After descending for 200 m, the track levels out and curves to the right. It drops down a little further before crossing a small stream. Beyond the stream, the footpath continues straight as the track bends round to the right.

WALK SIX - DETAIL MAP
First shorter variation

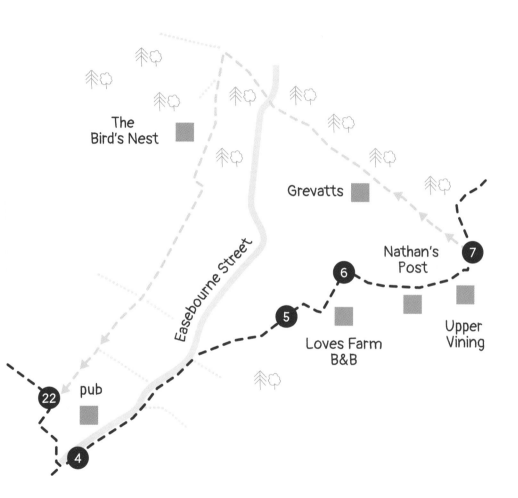

The Bird's Nest

Grevatts

Easebourne Street

Nathan's Post

7

6

5

Loves Farm B&B

Upper Vining

22

pub

4

A Cowdray notice just in front of the path marker warns walkers to keep to the footpaths, so make sure you leave the track at this point. The footpath is much narrower and steeper than the track and it ascends rapidly through mixed woodland and bracken.

The path has suffered a little from erosion, and one section is awkward to navigate as it cuts deeply into the hillside. Walkers have created a new path immediately to the left of the eroded section, and it is recommended that you use it.

9. At the top of the hill, the footpath meets a track. Turn right onto the track and then, after 150 m, go straight across a crossroad. Follow the path as it descends through the ancient woodland of Ovis Common. The trail is wide and signposted with the waymarkers for the Serpent Trail.

After 200 m, the trail comes alongside a post and rail fence. This is the boundary of the first of three properties on your right, and as you reach them, the path becomes a metalled track.

10. Remain on this track for 500 m until you come to another cluster of cottages on your right. This is Bexleyhill, and as you reach a white cottage, the track descends steeply to meet a road.

Turn left onto the road and follow it until you come to a property on your right called The Old Cottage. As you reach the end of its boundary fence, look for a wide grass track on the right. To access it, pass through a gap to the left of a green metal gate.

11. Follow this wide, well-signposted track through woodland that has pine trees to your right and coppice to your left. Once again, there are waymarkers for the Serpent Trail.

After 450 m, bear left to head steeply uphill into woodland that is used by mountain bikers. Keep to the footpath as it heads down and then up again, ignoring the bike trails to the left and the right. As you near the top of the second steep incline, the path turns sharply to the right and heads down again.

12. After 70 m, bear left at the fork and follow a level path through mixed woodland. Keep straight, ignoring smaller paths to the left and right. After 700 m, a wire fence appears on the left and several properties are visible ahead. This is Henley.

13. Keep the fence to your left and follow the path across a wooden boardwalk and then a wooden bridge over a small stream. On the far side of the bridge, go up a short flight of wooden steps, turning sharply left and then right before ascending another short flight of steps. The path narrows and has a boundary fence on either side. At the end of this path, turn right onto a track to pass a cluster of Cowdray cottages on your right.

The track ends at a tarmac road immediately opposite the car park for The Duke of Cumberland Arms public house. Turn left onto the road. Walk past the pub and continue ahead for 150 m until you come to a house and a footpath sign on the right.

If you would like to follow the second, shorter variation for this walk, continue along the road and follow the directions below. Otherwise, follow the path on the right across a wooden plank bridge and up a short flight of wooden steps. Crossing the driveway to the house, continue up another flight of steps and cross a stile to meet the A286.

Get Home Quicker ▶ As the road bends deeply to the right, look for a footpath on the left. Follow this path up a flight of wooden steps into woodland. Keep straight through the woods for 500 m, to arrive at a field. Head diagonally right across the field towards a gate on the opposite side.

As you cross the field, you are treated to some of the best views of Black Down anywhere in the area. Exit the field to make your way around the buildings of Verdley Farm, and then head down its driveway to a road. Turn left, and after 100 m, turn right onto a footpath. Follow this path for 350 m until you reach a crossroad. Turn right, and then after 200 m, turn left at a T-junction.

WALK SIX - DETAIL MAP
Second shorter variation

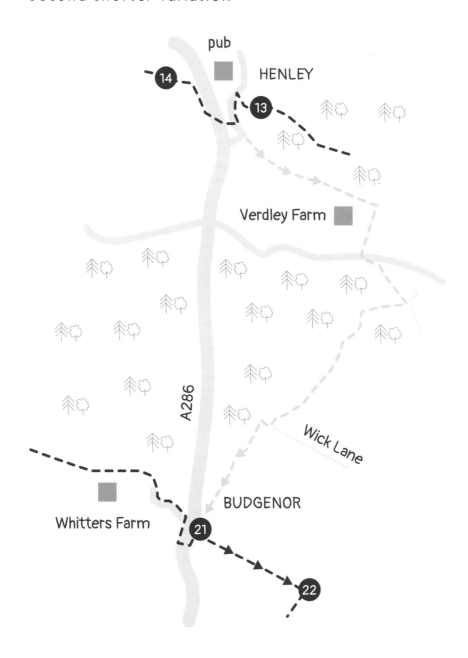

pub

HENLEY

14

13

Verdley Farm

A286

Wick Lane

Whitters Farm

BUDGENOR

21

22

Follow the woodland track for 900 m, then bear left at a fork. After 100 m, turn right at a T-junction, and then left at a second T-junction shortly after. Continue for 700 m, passing three cottages along the way. On the far side of the third cottage, take a footpath on the left to re-join the main route at Point **21.**

14.　Carefully cross the road to access a footpath directly opposite. This well-signposted woodland path heads downhill, above and parallel to the road. After 600 m, keep heading downhill as the path merges with another on your right.

Continuing down hill for another 300 m, the path eventually becomes a gravel driveway. Pass two cottages on the right and then turn sharp left at a T-junction. As soon as you make this turn, there is a third property on your right. This property is called Beeches Farm.

15.　Almost immediately, the path forks, and you need to bear right, staying close to the boundary of the farm. Ignore the first track off to the left but take the second to follow a signposted path that rises steeply through managed coppice.

As you climb higher, Black Down comes into view behind you. After 500 m, the path arrives at a T-junction. Turn left and then keep left at a fork to almost double back on yourself. Continue to climb uphill for another 20 m until you see a metal gate ahead.

As you reach the gate, turn right onto a track that runs along the edge of a field. After 150 m, there is a second metal gate. Cross the stile to the right of this gate and follow the track up a short slope into a field. Make your way across the middle of this field, heading towards the buildings of Scotland Farmhouse.

16.　With the buildings away to your left, cross the stile and follow the fence on your right for 20 m until you come to a track. Turn right onto this track and follow it as it bends sharply to the left. Continue ahead to arrive at a T-junction with a dirt road.

Stay Out Longer ▶ If you would like to extend the walk by joining it with Walk Five, turn right. After 250 m, look for signs on the left for the Serpent Trail. As you turn onto the Serpent Trail, look for the sandstone sculptures on either side of the path. These are referenced in Walk Five at Point **14.** Following the description in reverse from this point will lead you back to Midhurst via Older Hill, Iping, and Stedham.

To continue the main route, turn left on the dirt road and follow it until you come to an unmarked, off-road parking area on the right. Ignore the first entrance but take the second, and almost immediately, turn onto a footpath on the left that is signposted for the Lipchis Way.

17. Follow the path through woodland with a dry-stone wall to your left. You may recognise this part of the walk as it also features in Walk Five. After 400 m, keep left at a fork to take a faint path through the woods. Do not join the wider, signposted track 10 m ahead.

Keep left again after 70 m to take a sandy path out onto heathland that has heather and bracken to the left and right. Once again you are avoiding the wider track that runs parallel on your right. Continue across the open heath for 350 m. Keep straight at a footpath crossroad, and then after 30 m, turn left at a T-junction.

18.   After 100 m, go through a wooden gate to access the woodland of Lord's Common. To the right there is managed coppice and on the left is the boundary fence of the old King Edward VII Hospital. It is no longer a hospital and has recently been converted into private residences. As you head along the path, look out for glimpses of the distinctive and beautiful building through the trees.

The path meets the boundary of two detached properties 600 m after entering the woodland. At the far side of these properties, continue straight for another 200 m. Head across two footpath crossroads in quick succession. As you cross the second, the path becomes stony and uneven as it descends steeply.

19.   The path levels after 300 m and arrives at another footpath crossroads (although this one looks more like a lazy 'X' than a cross). Bear right on the signposted path. After 400 m, a track merges from the right. Continue on this track for another 400 m to arrive at a property on the left called Knighton's Well. Continue on the track, which is now a metalled road, to pass a cottage on the right.

20.   Follow the road as it heads downhill, and after 150 m, look for a short flight of steps on the left. Head up the steps and onto a footpath. This path skirts a property called Whitters Farm. The farmhouse and outbuildings are on the right. To your left is a field in which cattle are often grazed.

After passing Whitters farmhouse, the path descends steeply to a stile. Cross the stile and turn left onto a metalled road. Follow it around to the left, passing Budgenor Cottage, before arriving at a junction with the A286. Turn right at the junction, and after 100 m, cross over to double back down an access road beside the main road.

21.   Follow the access road for 100 m until you see a footpath sign pointing right. This is the point where the second, shorter variation re-joins the main route. Follow the path up a steep slope and out into open fields. Continue ahead as the path runs between two fields. Keep the hedgerows on your left as you follow the path for 500 m to arrive at a T-junction.

22.   This is where the first, shorter variation re-joins the main route. Turn right and head towards the the the far side of the field. As you get to the hedge, follow the path around to the left. Then take a path on the right to exit the field onto a track next to an allotment. Turn left on this track and follow it as it passes a graveyard.

Keep following the track as it becomes Glaziers Lane and bends first to the right and then to the left. After 100 m, the lane intersects with Easebourne Street, as noted in Point **3.** You are only 20 m away from the White Horse Pub and Easebourne village store.

Turn right and head to the junction with the A272. Cross the A272 and retrace your steps back through the churchyard and past Cowdray Farm Shop & Café.

From here, continue to retrace your steps on the track that runs beside the polo fields until you once again see Cowdray Ruins. Turn right in front of the ruins to take the causeway back into Midhurst via North Street Car Park.

Emerging from the car park onto North Street, turn left and continue past the shops until you come to Knockhundred Row. Turn left again and follow the road around to the right, past the museum and on towards the church and Market Square.

THE COWSHED AIRBNB

Tucked away down Carron Lane, just a few minutes from Midhurst town centre, is a hidden gem for those looking for a place to stay.

The Cowshed is a converted dairy barn and one of the oldest surviving buildings on this quiet residential lane. Completely self-contained, in a secluded location, and with a pretty courtyard garden, it is perfect for couples looking for a relaxing escape.

Quite how this quaint brick and timber barn survived as the properties of Carron Lane grew up around it is a bit of a mystery. It seems that, as the fields were developed for housing, the barn ended up on a plot with one of the homes. An enterprising former owner converted it, and current owner, Claire Daniels, has ploughed her energies into perfecting it as a vacation getaway.

Exquisitely decorated in tones of blue and grey, you feel calm and relaxed as soon as you step over the threshold. The layout is simple, with an open plan living space and doors leading from the bedroom out into the garden. The vaulted ceiling, skylights, and windows give the whole place a light and airy feel.

When The Cowshed opened its doors to guests back in 2016, the Daniels family had only recently moved into the main house. With two young children to look after, and no experience in holiday lettings, Claire looks back now and wonders how she managed. To guests and casual observers alike, the reason is clear. Her attention to detail and unwavering focus on providing a perfect experience are what makes a stay here so utterly enjoyable.

Claire is at the helm, but the rest of the family help whenever needed. As they live on the premises, you are guaranteed to be well looked after. Claire has even been known to pop guests in her own car to ensure they don't miss a train or bus connection.

Knowing that visitors will be looking forward to their stay keeps Claire firmly focussed on quality. From her comprehensive guide to the local area, to the spare toothbrushes, charging cables, and umbrellas left for you just in case it rains, she has tried to think of everything. Continuous improvement is Claire's mantra, and it shows in the care with which she looks after her guests. Keeping a low profile if she senses that guests would like privacy but ensuring she is available whenever needed is the sign of an experienced host, and Claire is certainly that.

Anyone who has stayed at The Cowshed will tell you they had an amazing time. You only need to glance at the Airbnb listing and its reviews to see how popular it is. You'll need to book well in advance or get lucky with a cancellation to stay here, but it is absolutely worth the wait.

THE ONE WITH
THE DISUSED RAILWAY

From the 1880s until the 1950s, Midhurst had no less than three branch lines servicing it. By 1955, they had all closed, the lines dismantled and the stations either demolished or repurposed.

Exploring the footpaths around Midhurst, you'll find lots of evidence of these branch lines, sometimes on private property and sometimes accessible. This walk shares the accessible parts of the Pulborough Line between Midhurst and Selham in the hopes that you will enjoy the slightly spooky yet nostalgic feeling that is characteristic of a walk on a disused railway line.

From Midhurst, the walk heads to the open access land beyond West Lavington to maximise the amount of time on the railway line. Following the line for 1.5 km, the route leaves the railway at the brilliantly named Little London. The irony is that there are only two cottages, so it is a very little London. From here, the route heads across Ambersham Common and then towards Selham, where there is a tiny Saxon church and a lovely pub.

A short section of the railway is accessible at Selham, and from its raised embankment, there are fine views across the Rother Valley. After leaving the Selham section of the railway line, you cross Graffham Nature Reserve before heading back to Ambersham Common. A final short stint on the railway ensures that the walk covers all the accessible sections. The route back to Midhurst is via Todham Rough and passes by the rear entrance to Cowdray House.

WALK SEVEN
➡ 17 km / ⏳ 5 hours

THE ONE WITH
THE DISUSED RAILWAY

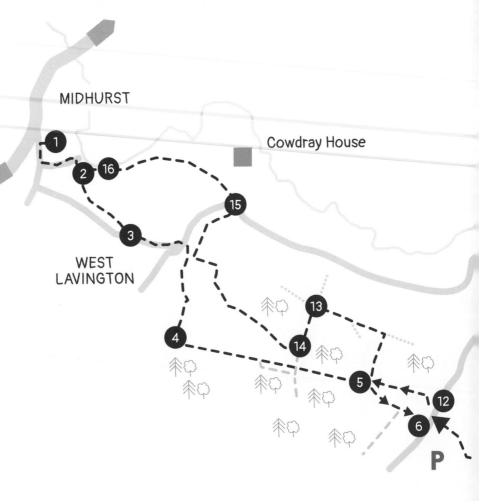

route guide 1

woods 🌲

site of interest ◼

P parking

walk route

alternative route

footpath/track

road

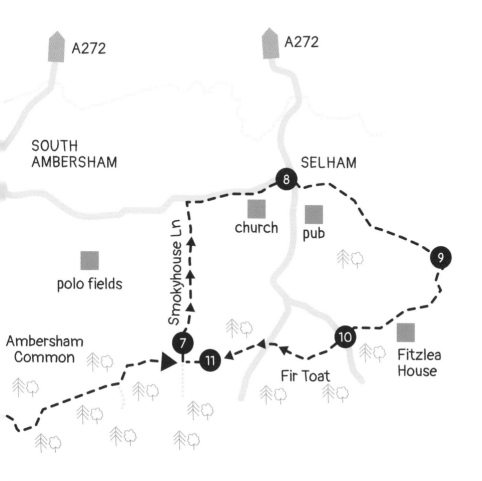

A272

A272

SOUTH
AMBERSHAM

SELHAM

8

church

pub

polo fields

Smokyhouse Ln

9

Ambersham
Common

7

11

10

Fitzlea
House

Fir Toat

➲ VARIATIONS

Several variations are provided. They include two shorter routes, as well as options to make the railway line more of a feature by repeating the section between West Lavington and Little London.

The shortest variation takes 1½ hours to complete, going only as far as the beautiful, red brick bridge in the middle of Todham Rough. A second, shorter variation turns back just as you reach Ambersham Common. This creates a route of around 2½ hours.

TAKE A FULL DAY TO EXPLORE

Options for extending the walk tend to turn it into a full day hike, and are not described in detail. Suggestions include making your way back from Selham via Lavington Common, Graffham, and even Heyshott. Alternatively, you could make your way from Selham to Petworth via Heath End and catch a bus back to Midhurst.

➲ AMENITIES

There is a delightful pub in Selham called The Three Moles. Although the pub itself is small, it has an extensive garden and makes for a lovely rest spot at what is roughly the mid-point of the walk.

There is also a serendipitous connection to the walk because, when the pub first opened in 1872, it was called 'The Railway Inn'. An attractive brick and tile hung building, standing high above the road, it was built to serve travellers on the railway.

➲ ROUTE GUIDE

1. From Market Square, face The Swan Inn and turn left to head down South Street. Take the first turning on the left into The Wharf. At the far end of this dead-end road, there is a stone bridge on the right. Cross the bridge and, keeping the Cowdray cottages on your left, head along the footpath.

2.   After 20 m, bear right at the fork to walk along the right-hand side of a field. The fence between you and the field is on your left. To your right there is woodland. Continue on this path for 500 m. After 200 m, you see a number of barns ahead, one of which has a distinctly Tudor look about it. As you reach the barns, follow the footpath around them and onto a country lane.

3.   Turn left onto the lane and follow it past a property called St. Andrews. Continue on down the hill until you pass a property on your right, called Coulter's Farm. Immediately after this property is a turning to the right. Head straight across the junction to access a gravel bridlepath signposted for Heyshott and Graffham.

Pass two cottages, noting the memorabilia in the garden of the second, and follow the path over a stream and around to the right. There is a steep wooded incline to the left and private gardens on the right. After 200 m, look out for a footpath heading steeply up on the left. This path has steep sides, and its lower section can get very boggy. Unlike other footpaths you encounter, there are few ways of negotiating the mud here. You may well need to head straight through it.

Follow the path for 100 m until you reach the top of the slope and a footpath crossroads. Turn right to enter a field. Turn right again to make your way around the edge of the field in an anti-clockwise direction. After 450 m, you arrive at the far right-hand corner of the field. Turn left to continue making your way around. There is an embankment on your right, and as you make your way along, the land gradually levels out. As it levels, look for a gap in the fence to exit the field and take your first steps onto the old railway line.

4.   What remains of the line stretches away to your left. Conversely, on your right, bushes and trees have covered any trace of the old railway. For all you can see, it might never have existed at all. Head left, along the line, for 700 m until you are almost about to pass underneath a beautiful red brick bridge. Unlike other bridges along the route, this one is complete, and it is possible to walk over it as well as under it.

If you want to keep the walk short, follow the directions below. To continue the main route, go under the bridge and stay on the railway line for a further 600 m to arrive at a footpath crossroads.

Get Home Quicker ▶ Before you get to the bridge, look to the right to find an unmarked path rising steadily up beside the line. This path is 100 m from the bridge itself and not signposted. Follow this path until it is level with the bridge. Turn left to cross over the bridge, and after 70 m, turn left again onto a wide track through the woods. Skip ahead to Point **14.** to follow the main route back to Midhurst.

5. Since the bridge, your path has been in a cutting, but as you reach the crossroads, the line stretches away on an embankment. You will get a chance to walk this section of the line on the return route. The path on your left is also part of the return route. For now, turn right to head down a track into woodland, ignoring the track that rises up on the right, heading back the way you came.

At the bottom of the slope, look back towards the railway line to see another fully intact, red brick bridge. Head away from this bridge to continue through the wood. The path curves deeply to the right, and at a T-junction on the far side of the bend, turn left. Head down a slope and, after 30 m, cross a wooden bridge. Beyond the bridge, follow the path around to the left, then keep left at a fork.

LITTLE LONDON'S PRIVATE RAILWAY

Follow the track as it heads towards a cottage on your left. As you reach its garage, there is a footpath crossroads ahead. Go straight across to pass a second cottage. These two cottages are the only properties in this tiny place, called Little London. Notice the train-related memorabilia in the garden of the second cottage. A yellow and green signal box is the most prominent, but there are other features, including railway tracks, signals, sidings, and engine sheds. Clearly an enthusiast lives (or lived) here.

6. The track you are on is much wider now and has been reinforced with red bricks. The bricks are remarkably similar to those used for the bridges seen earlier in the walk. Continue on the track for 350 m until you arrive at a road. As the road comes into view, note the track to your left. This is the route you will take on the return journey.

Before you reach the road, there is a footpath on the right, signposted for the Serpent Trail. This path is the start of the second, shorter variation. To take this route, follow the directions below. To continue the main route, cross the road, taking a footpath directly opposite to follow the Serpent Trail across Ambersham Common.

Get Home Quicker ▶ This variation follows the Serpent Trail's Tail Route for 1.7 km across Heyshott Common. There are many footpaths crossing the common, but the Serpent Trail is clearly marked. Trust in the waymarkers and you will arrive back at the first of the two red brick bridges that you saw earlier in the route.

There is only one point where you might feel you are losing the trail. It comes after 800 m, just as you re-enter the woods and arrive at a stream. Multiple paths converge here, but if you keep straight and cross the stream, you will see your next marker 20 m ahead. After another 900 m, you arrive at the bridge and can skip ahead to re-join the main route from Point **14.**

Make sure you follow the green waymarkers for the Serpent Trail's Head Route. After 100 m, you arrive at a T-junction near a small car park. Turn left, and after another 250 m, you arrive at a crossroad. Go straight across to follow a track along the edge of a clearing.

As the track bends deeply to the right, take the second turning on the left. This path quickly meets a crossroad. Head straight across and steeply down towards the woodland ahead. At the bottom of the slope there is a creek and the path is very sandy. Cross the creek and head into the woods. After 100 m, turn left to remain on the Serpent Trail.

WALK SEVEN - DETAIL MAP
Second shorter variation

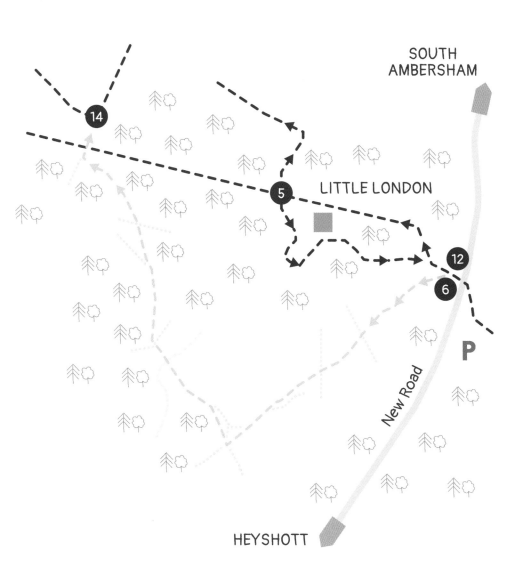

Make your way through the woods for 200 m until you emerge on the edge of a clearing. Keep to the tree line on the right with the clearing on your left. Beyond the tree line, there are fields.

As you reach the far side of the clearing, there is an outdoor, floodlit riding school on the right. Beyond this, the Serpent Trail continues straight ahead whilst you take a turning to the left.

You are once again in woodland with fields, just visible through the trees on the right. Keep straight for 250 m to arrive at a large field. Fences have been used to divide this field into four sections. Continue ahead with a field (and a fence) on either side of you. On the far side of the field there are woods. The return route will emerge from these woods later in the walk.

7. Before you reach the woods, there is a footpath crossroad. Turn left to pass a large green barn and follow the track down towards more buildings, crossing a ford on the way. Go through the wooden gate beside a house to access a metalled road. This is Smokyhouse Lane, and you follow it for 700 m until you come to a T-junction.

As you make your way along Smokyhouse Lane, you cross a bridge. This is another remnant of the old railway. The line is not accessible, or even visible here, but away to the left, on the far side of the South Ambersham polo fields, you can see a tree-lined embankment. There is also some evidence of the line on the right-hand side of the bridge. It used to track a course across the fields to Selham station.

When you reach the T-junction, turn right to head into Selham. After 300 m, you pass Selham Priory (now a residence), and 150 m further along, you come to Selham Church. The church dates back to the 11th century. It is small and incredibly pretty, with a distinctive, herringbone-pattern stonework on the wall that faces the road.

Continue past the church for 200 m until you come to a T-junction. Turn right, and after 30 m, you see the entrance to Hurlands Farm on the left. If you want to visit The Three Moles public house, continue along this road for 150 m. The pub is on the left, sitting high above the road.

8.   To continue the walk, turn left into Hurlands Farm and make your way across the yard. On the far side of the yard, follow a farm track as it bends to the right and heads between two fields. Keep going on this track for 400 m. As it is used by farm vehicles to access the fields, it can often be muddy.

On the far side of the fields, stay on the track to pass between the brick supports of an old railway bridge. Turn sharply to the left and head towards the large barn ahead. As you draw level with the barn, the track heads up an embankment and onto the railway line.

Make your way along the line for 500 m until you come to a crossroad with power lines running overhead. Walk under the power lines and head down the farm track on the right. Although the railway line is accessible for another 400 m, after this, it is on private land. Feel free to walk along it as far as the locked gates before retracing your steps and continuing the walk.

9. After leaving the railway line, make your way along the track, following it around a sharp left-hand bend. Then, 70 m after the bend, you arrive at a T-junction. This junction is on the apex of a deep bend. Turn right and follow the track around to the right. On the far side of the bend you see a property ahead on the left. Keep following the track until you arrive at a gate with a sign for Fitzlea House and Cottage. Ignore the track on the left just beyond the gate, and continue ahead for another 250 m until you come to a road.

GRAFFHAM'S NATURAL BEAUTY

10. Cross the road and go through a wooden gate into a wood called Fir Toat. This is part of the Graffham Nature Reserve and it is managed by the Sussex Wildlife Trust. Follow the wide grass track down through the wood for 250 m until you come to a clearing where several paths meet.

There is a wide sandy track on the left and another one straight ahead. There are two narrower paths to the right. Ignore the wide tracks and take the signposted footpath on the right.

The path quickly bends to the left and, beyond the bend, it becomes much wider. It then bends to the right, heads up steeply, and becomes quite sandy. After a final bend to the left, you see a wooden five bar gate ahead on the right.

Go through the gate to exit the nature reserve and make your way to the road, 50 m ahead. On the opposite side of the road there is a footpath. Cross the road and follow this path as it bends sharply to the left and then continues through the woods. After 300 m, turn left at a T-junction. You quickly arrive at a second T-junction, where you turn right.

After the right-hand turn, there are power lines running parallel to the path and fields beyond the woods ahead. Upon reaching the fields, go through a gate. The scene should look familiar. It is the large field, divided into four sections, that you walked across earlier. The large green barn and Smokyhouse Lane are away to your right. Head straight across the field to the crossroad.

TEST YOUR MEMORY

11.   Go straight across the crossroad to retrace your steps through the woods to the point where you previously left the Serpent Trail. You meet the trail again at a T-junction, 250 m after entering the woods. Keep straight as you make your way through the woods, ignoring two turnings to the right.

On arriving at the T-junction, turn right to follow the purple waymarkers for the Serpent Trail's Tail Route. Walk through the wood, over the creek, and across Ambersham Common, following the Serpent Trail all the way to the road.

This should take around 20 minutes. You have walked the route already, it should feel familiar, and the waymarkers are very clear.

You do need to keep alert after crossing the creek to make sure you are on the right path. Turn left to stay on the Serpent Trail; do not head straight onto a very similar looking, sandy path that also heads up the hill.

12.   When you reach the road, cross over and head along the wide track you walked previously. You now leave the Serpent Trail (which continues on a footpath to your left). Head straight for another 50 m before bearing right onto another wide track. The track bends to the left and after 100 m, arrives at a green metal gate. Go around the gate and turn left onto another section of the old railway line.

You are now (as promised) on the part of the line that runs behind the Little London cottages. If you are really keen to walk the whole length of this part of the line again, feel free to retrace your steps. Use the route guide in reverse from point **5**, back to the start of the walk. Alternatively, you could walk back as far as the bridge and, following the notes for the first, shorter variation, join the return route at point **14.**

To continue the main route, follow the line for 400 m until you once again come to a crossroad. Turn right to head away from the line and into the woods. Note that you are taking the opposite path from the one you took earlier, at Point **5.**

Follow a wide path away from the line. This path bends deeply to the right and then to the left. At the left hand bend, a path joins from the right. Keep heading away from the line to walk through the woods until you come to a T-junction. Turn left to walk along the edge of the wood, with fields on the right, beyond the tree line.

13. Keep to this path for 550 m until you arrive at a footpath crossroad. Half way along this route, the path will widen as a track merges from the left. When you reach the crossroad, turn left and head straight for 300 m to find a footpath sign pointing to the right.

LOOK DOWN ON THE TRACK

Before you take this path, keep straight for another 70 m to find yourself on the red brick bridge above the railway line. Take a look at your earlier route from this vantage point before turning back and taking the footpath you noted earlier (which is now on your left).

14. This is the point where both variations re-join the main route. The path begins as a wide track that is sometimes used by vehicles carrying out forest operations. It can be very muddy and is deeply rutted. After 200 m, keep straight, ignoring the turning to the left. The track gradually narrows beyond this point and starts to descend as it winds its way through the woods.

After 500 m, bear right at a fork on the corner of a clearing. Walk along the edge of the clearing, and after 100 m, bear left at a second fork. Continue on this path for 150 m until you come to a T-junction right on the edge of an extremely steep slope.

Turn right to make your way out of the woods and along the edge of a field. After 250 m, the path heads down below the level of the field and onto a road.

15. Turn left onto the road and head towards what looks like a crossroad. In reality it is a hairpin bend, with the rear entrance to Cowdray House on the right and an access road straight ahead. The access road leads to Kennels Dairy, which is no longer in use. Follow this road for 250 m, until you reach the dairy.

Head straight, along a wide concrete road, between two stable blocks. Keep close to the stables on your left. The other stables and dairy buildings are away to your right. After passing the last of the buildings on the left (which is a Cowdray cottage), exit the dairy premises onto a footpath.

The footpath runs between two fields, and after 250 m, the field on your right is replaced by trees. Beyond the trees the land drops away steeply down to the polo fields behind Cowdray Ruins. It is possible to catch glimpses of the ruins through the trees.

16. After 450 m, the path heads down steeply and another path merges from the left. This is the path you took at the start of the walk. Turn right to pass, once again, in front of the Cowdray cottages. Cross over the stone bridge and turn left to retrace your steps back down The Wharf. Turn right onto South Street to make your way back to Market Square.

CLICKABLE MIDHURST

Not all businesses in Midhurst have a high street presence. There are local artisans working away to build viable businesses online. Unless you're around when they set up shop at a local market or an event, you could miss them entirely, which would be a shame, for you, and for them. Here are two of these online businesses to get you started.

JULIET ROSE (MORE THAN JUST SOAPS)

Juliet began her business journey almost two decades ago when she suddenly started losing her hair and switched to natural shampoos and conditioners in a bid to solve the problem. Delighted with the results and curious to know more, Juliet started making her own hair care products.

"Nowadays, it is more common to find shampoo and conditioner sold as a solid bar wrapped in paper rather than as a liquid in a plastic bottle, but back then it was a real novelty." recalls Juliet.

For someone as inquisitive and creative as Juliet, it was only a matter of time before she branched out into other beauty products. Entire ranges of haircare, skincare, perfume, and candles now come under the Juliet Rose brand, and all are made at her home in Midhurst.

Juliet's business is as plastic-free and environmentally friendly as possible. She uses natural ingredients for all her products. Most of the work is done by Juliet herself. Not only does she make all the products, she also designs the labels, You can see her full range at: **julietrosesoaps.com**

JO CRAIG (MIDHURST FLOWER FARM)

Cut flowers are big business, with a big environmental impact. Jo's mission is to bring us all back to nature. Using organic flower farming methods and homemade feeds, Jo is forging a new approach to having seasonal, cut flowers in your home.

When you buy from Jo, you know you're buying direct from the grower and that the flowers have been lovingly tended on her plot just minutes from the centre of Midhurst. You are also benefitting from Jo's extraordinary flair for creating beautiful arrangements in simple and sustainable ways.

Choose to buy whenever you see Jo's stall in town or sign up for regular deliveries at **midhurstflowerfarm.com**. Out of season, while Jo is busy preparing her plot, you can enjoy her dried flowers, table decorations, and seasonal wreaths.

THE ONE WITH THE LOST VILLAGES

It is estimated that there are around 3,000 lost villages across England. Most were abandoned during the 14th or 15th century due to either the Black Death or changes in land use. Across Sussex, there are many such villages, and this walk takes you right to the foot of the South Downs to visit one. Two more are nearby and can be visited as extensions to the main route.

From Midhurst, you head through woodland towards Minsted and out onto farmland. The majority of the walk is across farmland, mostly arable with some livestock. As you make your way across this flat but attractive landscape towards Treyford, you are heading straight towards the South Downs. Treyford Hill suddenly dominates as you emerge onto a country lane beside a cluster of cottages.

A CHURCHYARD WITH NO CHURCH

A short diversion enables you to visit the derelict 13th century church of St Mary's, as well as the churchyard of the demolished 19th century St. Peter's. This tiny village, although not technically a lost village, does have two lost churches.

Heading across farmland at the foot of the Downs, you arrive in Didling. This is thought to be a lost village, and right at the bottom of Didling Hill is the only remaining structure, the shepherd's church of St. Andrew.

From here, you can extend the walk to visit two more lost villages, Linch and Bepton. There is very little to see at Linch today, other than a farm, but Bepton still has a church (St. Mary's), and in the churchyard there is a mass grave of plague victims.

The main route continues across farmland back to Minsted. This tiny hamlet grew relatively recently out of a series of renovations and conversions. Old stone barns and farm cottages are now family homes, lining the track that leads to fields, in which there are crops and a small herd of dairy cows. In contrast with the lost villages of Bepton, Linch, and Didling, you could say that Minsted was a 'found' village; a 20th century creation conveniently illustrating the changing use of land and property over time.

Over 75% of the South Downs National Park is farmed. It has been farmed for centuries, and this has shaped the terrain we see today. Whilst the fields are larger than they used to be, the patchwork effect of land divided by hedgerows has not been lost. The scenery is beautiful because it is cultivated, not in spite of it. Framed by the Downs and inhabited by a wide variety of wildlife, this landscape is as alluring as any shared in this book.

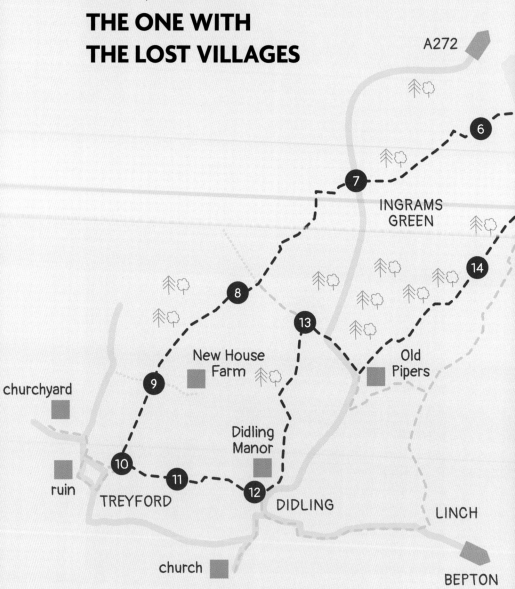

WALK EIGHT
➤ 18 km / ⏳ 5¼ hours

THE ONE WITH
THE LOST VILLAGES

A272

6

7

INGRAMS
GREEN

14

8

13

New House
Farm

Old
Pipers

churchyard

9

Didling
Manor

10   11   12

ruin

TREYFORD   DIDLING

LINCH

church

BEPTON

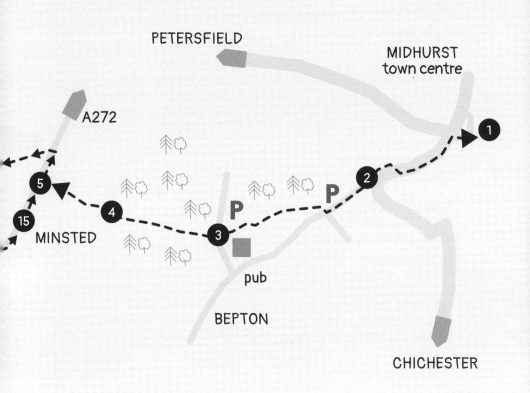

PETERSFIELD

MIDHURST
town centre

A272

1

2

5

4

15

3

MINSTED

P

P

pub

BEPTON

CHICHESTER

1	route guide		walk route
🌲	woods		alternative route
◼	site of interest		footpath/track
P	parking		road

➲ VARIATIONS

Two variations are provided. One enables the route to be shortened; the other extends the walk to include the lost village of Linch. There are also options to explore the ruined church and cemetery at Treyford, as well as the shepherd's church at the foot of the Downs near Didling.

The shorter route takes a path across fields just outside the hamlet of Ingram's Green. It excludes the villages of Treyford and Didling but it is nonetheless a pleasant countryside route. It takes around 3 hours to complete.

Directions are provided for the extension to Linch, and this route is shown on the map. Note that this extension includes a section along a country road that may not be suitable for everyone. If you are feeling particularly energetic, you could extend your walk as far as St. Mary's Church in Bepton. This prolongs the amount of time walking along a country road, but you can take a footpath route back to Minsted. This route is shown on the extension map.

➲ AMENITIES

Whilst there are plenty of amenities in Midhurst at the start and end of the walk, there are no amenities on the route itself. You could make a diversion from Treyford to visit the Three Horseshoes in Elsted, but this would add an extra 3 km to the walk. You could also make a diversion to The Country Inn in Bepton, which adds only a few hundred metres to the walk.

➲ ROUTE GUIDE

1. With Garton's Coffee House on your left, go around the left of The Swan Inn to head along West Street. Follow it to the junction with Bepton Road and turn left. Cross over at the pedestrian crossing to walk along Bepton Road for 600 m until it curves sharply to the left and becomes New Road.

2.   Continue straight as the main road bends to the left to remain on Bepton Road. Walk on the left-hand side of the road as there is no pavement on the right. After 350 m, cross the road to access a footpath beside a small parking area.

Follow the wide woodland path for 550 m until it bends sharply right to pass through a cutting in the embankment of a disused railway. If you look carefully as you pass through the cutting, you can see what remains of the brick supports of an old railway bridge. Bear left at the fork 20 m after the cutting and continue for 200 m until you arrive at a car park beside Severals Road.

3.   Make your way across the car park and over the road onto a track beside a property called Oakwood House. Opposite the gates of the house is a footpath. Bear right onto the path and follow it for 700 m until you come to a T-junction. Turn right, and after 100 m, cross a concrete bridge over a small stream. Go through the metal gate on the far side of the bridge to exit the woodland.

4.   Ahead are the open fields of Minsted Farm. Cross a small area of rough ground to pass through a gate into these fields. With the hedgerows on your right, continue ahead until you come to two metal five bar gates. Navigate around the gates (they are sometimes open, sometimes closed) and follow the track ahead to pass in front of two cottages.

Outside the second cottage is an old shepherd's hut on wheels (as pictured in Walk Three). After passing the shepherd's hut, the track bends deeply to the left before bending right and coming to a T-junction with Minsted Road. Looking to the left down Minsted Road, you see a clusters of houses in the distance. You will return along this road at the end of the walk.

5.   Turn right onto the road and continue straight for 200 m. Ignore the first footpath on the left (after 80 m) and take the second, also on the left. This is a wide, tree-lined path. The fir trees meet overhead, making it dark, even on a sunny day. It feels as though you are walking through a green tunnel.

After 300 m, the green tunnel ends. Keep straight, past a footpath on the left to head slightly uphill on a path that is much narrower than before. There is a fence and overgrown hedgerows to the right. On the left there is a field. After another 150 m, the path heads into a wood. The hedgerows on the left are replaced by rhododendron bushes, and you can no longer see the field.

6. Continue through the wood for 400 m. The path here is always muddy but you can navigate around the mud using the little "rabbit runs" on the left that have been worn by walkers. Keep straight as you pass two footpaths in quick succession, both heading off to the right.

Ahead there are fields and views towards the South Downs. Exit the woodland and follow the path as it curves deeply to the right between two fields. There are often horses in these fields, and sometimes there are sheep in the field to your left.

LARGE POND, OR SMALL LAKE?

As you come to the edge of the field on your left, you arrive at a T-junction. Ahead is a property called Fitzhall Cottage. Turn left to walk between its garden and the field on your left. Look out for the large pond at the far end of the garden.

Beyond the pond, the path skirts Henfield Wood. The woodland itself is on the right, and beyond the trees on your left lies farmland. After 700 m, the path meets Ingram's Green Lane.

7. Cross the lane to pass through the metal gate opposite. Follow a grass track straight across a field. This is the point where the route becomes a journey across many fields. If you complete the full route, you will encounter 20 fields in total before arriving back in Minsted.

On the far side of the field, go through another metal gate to follow a path along the edge of another field. There is a high wire deer fence on your right.

After 200 m, turn right to pass through another metal gate. This enables you to continue following the high wire fence. Ahead is what remains of a disused railway. Pass between the red brick supports, for what was once a bridge, and continue to follow the fence for a further 125 m.

Keep straight as the fence heads to the right, passing through a metal gate. Turn to your left to make your way around the edge of a field. After 300 m, there is a signed footpath crossroad. If you want to follow the shorter variation, turn left. To continue the main route, go straight across. Note that, depending on the time of year, the path on the right at this crossroads may not be very easy to see.

Get Home Quicker ▶ Follow the track (also known as Brimbrook Lane) for 400 m to arrive at another footpath crossroad. Head straight across to re-join the main route at Point **13.** (note, the main route joins from the footpath on the right, at the crossroad).

8. Continue for 200 m past the footpath crossroad to arrive at the corner of the field. Turn right to keep following the path around the edge of the field. After 50 m, turn left to exit the field, crossing a stream and passing through a metal gate as you do so.

Follow a grass track straight across the field ahead of you, keeping to the right of a stream and two trees. Exit the field via a gate and cross a patch of rough ground before passing through a gap in a fence to enter another field. Walk across this field to a double set of metal gates on the opposite side.

As you pass through these gates, you enter the first of two fields that are often used to graze sheep. New House Farm is away to your left, and ahead on the right is a short row of cottages. Go straight across both fields (450 m) until you come alongside the cottages. Ahead is a wide dirt track. Exit onto the track and turn right to walk across a cattle grid. Immediately after the cattle grid, on the opposite side of the track, there is a wooden 'kissing gate'.

9.　Go through the gate and make your way across a small field towards another gate. After passing through the second gate, there are telephone wires running above and slightly to the right of the footpath. These wires will keep you on track as you cross the fields ahead and make your way towards Treyford. After 150 m, hedgerows appear on your right. Keep straight to go through a gap in a post and wire fence ahead.

Keep following the footpath and the overhead wires to make your way along the side of a narrow valley. The valley falls away to your left and the hedgerows continue close by on your right. As you come to the gap in a second post and wire fence, keep straight to pass under the telephone wires and on towards the wooden panel fence of a property called Mill House. As you reach the fence, turn sharply to the right to pass through a metal gate.

Follow the footpath along the boundary of Mill House. After 10 m, the fence gives way to a beech hedge. After another 20 m, you are at the corner of the property, and the path makes a sharp turn to the left. Pass in front of the house and then head down a short but very steep slope onto a single-track road.

This is Treyford, a small village nestling at the foot of the South Downs. Treyford Hill rises so majestically above the cottages, they look for all the world as though they are huddling together for safety. If you would like to visit the cemetery and the ruined church, turn right and follow the variations below. Otherwise, turn left past the gate of Mill House and onto the gravel driveway of the neighbouring property, called The Studio. To continue the main route, skip ahead to Point **10.**

See The Churchyard　▶　Follow the single-track road up to meet a T-junction. Turn right, and after 100 m, take the turning on the left. After 150 m, turn right to access the churchyard via a gate. When you have visited the churchyard, either retrace your steps or visit the ruins of St. Mary's church, as described below.

WALK EIGHT - DETAIL MAP
Treyford

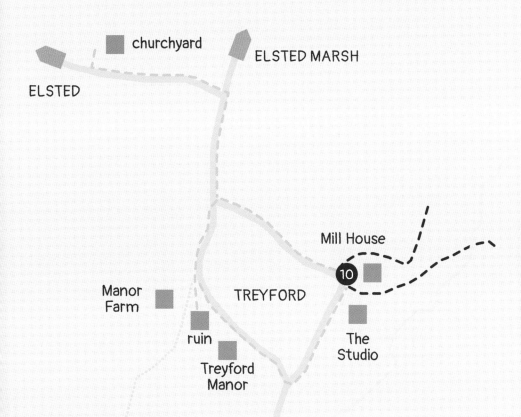

churchyard

ELSTED MARSH

ELSTED

Mill House

Manor
Farm

TREYFORD

10

ruin

The
Studio

Treyford
Manor

DIDLING

Visit The Ruined Church ▶ If you are visiting the church after seeing the churchyard, retrace your steps to the T-junction and turn right. After 100 m, keep straight as you come to the single-track road that leads down to Mill House. If you have not visited the churchyard and only want to see the ruins, make your way up the single-track road from Mill House and turn left at the T-junction.

Ahead on the right is the entrance to Manor Farm. As you arrive at the entrance, the road makes a sharp turn to the left. Look for an unmarked footpath leading up from the road. The remains sit above the road, but the site can get overgrown. The route in is not always particularly obvious, and it is not signposted.

Explore the ruins and then retrace your steps back to the road. You can either go back the way you came or turn right to walk down the road, past the entrance to Treyford Hall. Turn left at the bottom of the hill to walk past several cottages until you see Mill House ahead. Turn right on the gravel driveway that leads to a property called The Studio and re-join the main route at Point **10.**

10.   After passing the entrance to The Studio, the footpath narrows and heads downwards, with hedges on either side. After 75 m, the hedges give way to woodland. Continue through the woods for 100 m until you arrive at a wooden gate. Cross a small, stone bridge and go through the gate. You now face a steep climb up a flight of wooden steps. After 15 m, there is another gate. Go through and continue your climb to the top of the steps.

As you reach the top of the steps, you emerge from woodland into a field. Keep straight, with the hedgerows on your right, and after 150 m, look out for a wooden gate on the right. Go through the gate and turn to your left to continue along the edge of a field, this time with the hedgerows on your left. You now have uninterrupted views across to the South Downs. Treyford Hill is right beside you. In the distance, you see Didling Hill and the tiny white church that sits on the hill's lower slopes.

11. Keep straight for 700 m to pass across three fields. Exit the first of the three fields via a wooden gate. As you go through, turn to your left to follow the hedgerows around the edge of the field in a clockwise direction. After 50 m, you reach the corner of the field. Turn right to keep to the hedgerows on your left.

After 75 m, the path heads down into the far corner of the field. In this corner, there is a double set of gates that lead into the third field. Pass through the first gate and then cross a stile beside the second. Turn right to follow the hedgerows in an anticlockwise direction around the edge of the field. After 100 m, turn left at a footpath sign to head up a slope and across the middle of the field.

The footpath is not visible at this point because the ground is too rough and the path is not well established. Strike a straight line, and as you climb higher up the slope, a number of buildings come into view ahead. Maintain a straight line towards the buildings, making sure the large, modern barns are on your left.

Exit the field via a wooden gate to access a large concrete yard. Before you go through the gate, take a moment to look around. The views of the South Downs have already been noted, but from this vantage point there are lovely views in almost every direction.

Make your way across the yard to pass through a second wooden gate and onto an access road. Continue straight for another 50 m until the access road meets a country lane. To visit the shepherd's church of St. Andrew, turn right and follow the directions below. Also turn right if you want to extend the route to Linch. Otherwise, turn left, and continue the main route at Point **12.**

Visit The Shepherd's Church ▶ To visit the church, keep straight for 350 m, continuing past a turning on the left and arriving at a sharp right-hand bend. Continue straight to leave the road for a wide dirt track. Follow the track for 150 m to find the church on your right. Retrace your steps to continue the main route.

WALK EIGHT - EXTENSION MAP
Linch and Bepton

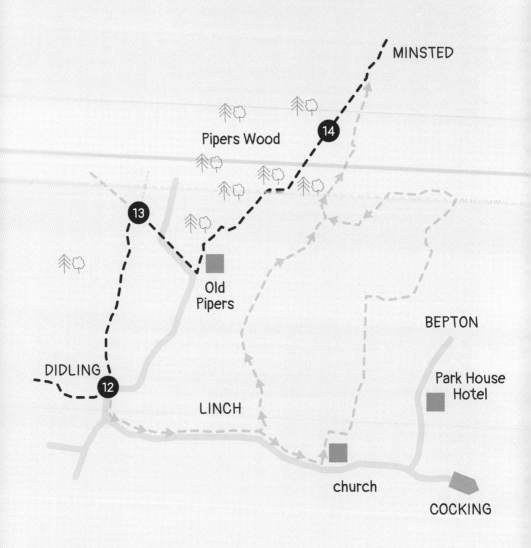

MINSTED

Pipers Wood

14

13

Old
Pipers

BEPTON

Park House
Hotel

DIDLING

12

LINCH

church

COCKING

Stay Out Longer ▶ To extend the route to Linch or Bepton, head down the road for 130 m and take the turning on the left (Bugshill Lane). Follow it for 1 km to get to Linch. To get to Bepton, continue on Bugshill Lane for another 800 m before turning left to find the church. Unfortunately, there are no footpaths leading directly from Didling to Linch or Bepton. When you are ready, you can retrace your steps to continue the main route or follow the footpaths shown on the extension map. Following the footpaths from Linch or St. Mary's Bepton enable you to reconnect with the main route just outside Minsted. These variations will extend the walk quite significantly. Expect to be out for at least another 2 hours.

12. Follow the road as it curves to the right, past the entrance to Didling Manor. Note the three pairs of Grade II listed gate posts as you pass by. On the far side of the bend, take the track on the left to pass a property called Coronation Villa. As you pass the front door of a second property called Old Cottage, bear right to follow a footpath around to the rear of a garage. Once you are on the far side of the garage, continue through a gate into the field ahead.

Keep to the edge of this field, with the hedgerows on your left. After 120 m, keep straight, ignoring the footpath on the left. Continue along the edge of the field for another 300 m to head down towards a metal gate. Go through the gate and across the next field to a double set of gates on the far side. Go through both gates to access a large field.

It is likely that this field was once three separate fields. It looks as though the hedgerows have been removed, but the drainage ditches and some of the trees have been retained. Keep to the right until you have crossed the first ditch. Then head diagonally left across the second and third sections of the field towards a metal gate in the far left-hand corner.

Go through this gate and turn right onto a wide track. This track is known as Brimbrook Lane and is the point where the short variation re-joins the main route.

13. Head along the track for 200 m until it meets a road. Bear right onto the road and follow it for 300 m. As the road makes a sharp turn to the right, head left beside a property called Old Pipers. Continue along this track for 150 m, passing a wooden-clad bungalow along the way. As the track makes a sharp turn to the right to pass in front of two wooden garages, look for a footpath on the left. The path is narrow and hard to see, as it runs down the side of the left-hand garage to give access to Pipers Wood.

Keep straight through the woods on a wide track for 200 m. Bear right at a footpath sign, and after another 70 m, exit the woods into a long, narrow field. Turn to your left and keep to the edge of the field for 250 m. Then follow a diagonal path through the grass towards a gate on the opposite side.

Go through the gate and into woodland again. Follow a wide track through the wood, bearing left after 175 m. After another 120 m, exit the wood and keep straight along the edge of a field, with hedgerows and woodland on your left.

14. After 100 m, cross the wooden bridge on your left to make your way across what remains of a disused railway line. Head down the old embankment, turning right at the bottom of the slope. Almost immediately, turn left to head up the embankment on the opposite side. At the top of the slope, cross a stile to access a field.

Bear slightly right across the field to the woods opposite. Cross another stile and then a wooden bridge to enter the woods. Follow the path through the woods for 140 m to emerge once again into a field. At the entrance to this field there is a stile but there is no longer a gate beside it, so you can simply make your way through the gap in the hedgerows.

There is no visible footpath across this field. The ground is uneven and muddy in places. It is often used to graze cattle. Bearing slightly right, head across the field. As you near the middle, you see a stone bridge on the far side. Head towards this bridge and exit the field via the metal gate next to it.

Turn left onto a dirt track. Cross the bridge and continue for 180 m until you arrive at the first property in Minsted. This property is on your right and is called Minsted Old House. Continue along the track, which is now more of a road, for another 300 m until you arrive at the entrance to Minsted farm.

15. Continue along the road, past the farm entrance, for another 150 m, before turning right onto a track. You can now retrace your steps along the route you took at the start of the walk. Follow the track round to the left, then right, and then left again to pass the shepherd's hut and cottages. Navigate the metal gates to access the right-hand field ahead, making sure to keep the fence on your left.

On the far side of the field, pass through a gate into a rough, grassed area. Head towards the woods, through a gate, and over a concrete bridge. After 100 m, turn left onto a long, straight path through the woods. Continue on this path for 700 m to emerge from the woods beside Oakwood House and Severals Road.

Cross the road and the small car park opposite. Go through the gap to the left of a metal gate and follow an uneven path up to a footpath sign. Turn right and make your way down a short, steep slope with the sides of an old embankment to the left and right. As you emerge from the embankment, turn left on a wide, woodland track. Stay on this track for 550 m until you come to Bepton Road.

Turn left onto Bepton Road, crossing over to walk on the pavement on the opposite side. After 350 m, you will come to the junction with New Road. Cross the junction to retrace your steps along the left-hand side of Bepton Road towards Midhurst town centre. Cross at the traffic lights and make your way into West Street. Continue straight along West Street to arrive back at Market Square.

NEXT STEPS AND FURTHER READING

If this book has inspired you to walk more often and explore your local footpaths more fully, a good 'next step' would be to get more familiar with maps. Whether you choose to view them online or in paper form, Ordnance Survey's 1:25,000 scale maps are perfect for designing your own routes.

Ordnance Survey's online App enables you to create routes, as well as estimate distances and durations. It plots elevations so you can see the intensity of ascents and descents. When out walking, the App tracks your position and lets you know if you have strayed from your chosen route. There is an annual subscription fee to access all the features on the App, but it's worth it if you want the confidence of knowing exactly where you are when you are exploring.

Investing in paper maps is a good move if you are keen to design a lot of walks. They will provide a useful back-up in case you lose access to any online resources you are using while you're out and about. You may be surprised by how pleasurable it is to pore over a map, working out the best way to connect footpaths, to get from one destination to another.

If you are ready to get more familiar with maps, OS Maps (**ordnancesurvey.com**) or Outdooractive (**outdooractive.com**) are just two of several online Apps you could try. The Ramblers Association (**ramblers.org.uk**) also have an App called 'Ramblers Routes', which offers any walking route under 3 miles for free, regardless of whether you are a member or not. All routes are free if you are a member. This is not unusual; most online walking apps offer access to a database of ready-made routes.

FINDING WALKING ROUTES

If you prefer to continue following ready-made walking routes, there are a number of free and subscription-based walking websites you can explore. 'Fancy Free' (**fancyfreewalks.org**) is one of the best of the free websites and definitely worth a try. Local newspapers and magazines often include walking routes as a regular feature and are also worth looking out for.

A rewarding option is to challenge yourself to complete some of the UK's Long Distance Paths (LDPs). These are maintained, waymarked routes that are upwards of 32 km in length. You can have fun working out how to split them to make them manageable, tackling them over several days or across a series of weekends. The Long Distance Walkers Association (**ldwa.org.uk**) has an online database of all LDPs in the UK.

If you are walking more frequently and over greater distances, you may want to invest in shoes, clothes, and equipment specifically designed for the outdoors. It can be daunting to know where to start, but there are plenty of places to seek advice.

WHAT GEAR IS BEST?

You could search online for reviews. There are plenty of vloggers and bloggers with outdoor-related content. Abbie Barnes is one of the best vloggers when it comes to gear reviews. Take a look at her website **spendmoretimeinthewild.co.uk** to find links to her YouTube channel (for her gear reviews), as well as podcasts, and event listings.

You can also find good advice in outdoor clothing outlets on the high street. Many high street stores have knowledgeable staff ready to help you choose the kit that's right for your needs. Cotswold Outdoor are particularly good. Most have online stores too, where you can benefit from customer reviews. For discounted items from most of the major brands try: **gooutdoors.com**

EARLY BIRD

One of the very best times of day to go walking is early in the morning, and one hour either side of sunrise is perfect for seeing wildlife and for getting great photos. Depending on the time of year, this doesn't mean that you have to get up super early, but you still might find it hard to entice others out with you.

Walking on your own can be daunting, but it is something that many people enjoy. Planning a route carefully before you set out or doing a walk you know well are good ways to feel confident on your own. Taking a mobile phone and letting someone know where you are going and when you expect to be back are important safety considerations, as is taking a basic first aid kit and some extra clothing in case you need to rest or wait for help.

SAFETY FIRST

You could also take a look at the website **what3words.com** to see how you could get help in an emergency. Planning to meet up with others part way round your walk is a really nice way to involve friends and family who are not keen to make early starts or are not able to complete lengthy routes.

Joining a local walking group is a good way to inspire you to get out and about regularly. Alongside well-known groups, such as The Ramblers Association, there are lots of other local groups you might choose to join. The University of the Third Age (**u3a.org.uk**) is particularly good, with many U3As offering regular, organised walks for anyone who is no longer in full-time work.

LIMBER DOWN

If you're walking regularly and clocking up long distances, you may find it helpful to build some stretching activities into your routine. One of the best ways to relax and stretch after a walk is to do a little yoga.

There are a number of ways you could do this, but one of the easiest is to follow an online instructor. There is a huge resource of free classes on YouTube, and some of the best are created by Adriene Mishler of 'Yoga With Adriene'. With plenty of short practices, targeting specific needs, you are sure to find something that appeals. Try 'Yoga for Tired Legs' to get you started.

KEEP IN TOUCH

To keep up to date with news and reviews related to the walks and articles in this book - visit: **findingfootpaths.com** New content is uploaded regularly and you can subscribe to be the first to know about events, such as guided walks, talks and competitions. Also, find out more about the second book in the Finding Footpaths series, due in early 2023.

ABOUT MICHELE

Michele lives in Midhurst with her partner, Andy, and two cats. She is passionate about walking, and for more than 10 years has walked extensively on the footpaths around Midhurst, building confidence in solo walking, map reading, and navigation.

She particularly enjoys long walks, which is why there are so many options in this book to extend the routes. In summer, Michele will often be up and out at sunrise and will happily complete a 20 km walk before breakfast!

Andy walks only as a last resort, so Michele almost always walks solo, but the pair do enjoy cycling together, although Michele finds this mode of transport a bit fast for her liking.

ACKNOWLEDGEMENTS

There are so many people to thank. I really hope I don't miss anyone out. Firstly, I'd like to thank the team that made the production of this book possible. Maddy Glenn of Softwood Self Publishing, Claire Smith of Booksmith Design and Julia Hughes of Hooli. Without the help of these talented women, this book would never have made it to print.

The inspiration for the book came from spending a lot of time watching YouTube. In particular, Athena Mellor, Abbie Barnes and Claire Beare. All of whom are inspiring women. Without knowing it, they have encouraged me in my walking, my photography, and above all my writing.

A lot of folks encouraged me once they knew what I was doing. Special thanks go to Jo Craig, who has been one of my biggest supporters. Also, Simon Wheeler who has given me valuable advice about bringing the book to market. I also had help from friends when I was making early decisions about the Finding Footpaths brand especially, Jane, Gavin, Sarah and Brian. Then there were the Midhurst business owners who let me pester them for photos and interviews: Brendon, Jamie, Claire, Digby, Jo, Juliet, Neil and Teresa. Also, employees at the South Downs National Park Authority who have been so helpful Zara, Charlie and Ruth.

Finally, to my long suffering partner Andy. He's cheerfully put up with me leaving him on his own for months whilst I was writing, checking the routes, and editing photographs. His cooking skills have improved enormously. I'm not so sure about the washing up though.

MORE WALKS
ARE ON THE WAY....

Sign up to my mailing list to be the first to hear.

Go to: **findingfootpaths.com**

Follow my footsteps:

on Instagram **@michele.facer**

on Twitter **@michele_facer**

join my "**Finding Footpaths**" Facebook group